DATE DUE

DEMCO 38-296

EUROPEANIZING GREECE:
THE EFFECTS OF TEN YEARS
OF EU STRUCTURAL FUNDS, 1989–1999

European Union Studies

European Union Studies features the latest research on topics in European integration in the widest sense, including Europe's role as a regional and international actor. This interdisciplinary series publishes the research of Canadian and international scholars and aims at attracting scholars working in various disciplines such as economics, history, law, political science, and sociology. The series is made possible in part by a generous grant from the European Commission.

The first series of its kind in Canada, and one of only a few in North America, *European Union Studies* is unique in looking at the EU 'from the outside,' making sense not only of European integration but also of the role of the European Union as an international actor.

GENERAL EDITORS:

Jeffrey Kopstein
Professor of Political Science
Director, Centre for European, Russian, and Eurasian Studies
University of Toronto

Amy Verdun
Professor of Political Science
Director, Jean Monnet Centre of Excellence
University of Victoria

For a list of books published in the series, see page 123.

NANCY A. VAMVAKAS

Europeanizing Greece

The Effects of Ten Years
of EU Structural Funds, 1989–1999

UNIVERSITY OF TORONTO PRESS
Toronto Buffalo London

ISBN 978-1-4426-4141-9

Printed on acid-free, 100% post-consumer recycled paper
with vegetable-based inks.

Library and Archives Canada Cataloguing in Publication

Vamvakas, Nancy A., 1967–
Europeanizing Greece : the effects of ten years of EU structural funds,
1989–1999 / Nancy A. Vamvakas.

(European Union studies)
Includes bibliographical references.
ISBN 978-1-4426-4141-9

1. European Union – Greece. 2. Greece – Politics and government – 1974–
3. Economic assistance, European – Greece. I. Title. II. Series: European
Union studies.

HC240.25.G8V34 2012   320.9495'09049   C2012-900027-2

University of Toronto Press acknowledges the financial assistance to its
publishing program of the Canada Council for the Arts and the Ontario
Arts Council.

 Canada Council Conseil des Arts
for the Arts du Canada

 ONTARIO ARTS COUNCIL
CONSEIL DES ARTS DE L'ONTARIO

University of Toronto Press acknowledges the financial support of the
Government of Canada through the Canada Book Fund for its publishing
activities.

To my parents, Roula and Agapios Vamvakas

Contents

Acknowledgments

I would like to thank officials in the Ministry of National Economy and the Ministry of the Interior in Athens for their assistance in the pursuit of this work. Also, politicians and public servants in the regional administrations (*perifereies* and prefectures) were more than generous with their time.

Further, I would like to thank officials in the Regional Directorate of the European Commission, and Anastasios Bougas in particular, for assisting me in collecting data and for offering me space to work in Brussels.

The European University Institute in Florence, Italy, was a gracious host.

Financial support was provided by the Social Sciences and Humanities Research Council through the Major Collaborative Research Initiatives Program.

Finally, a warm thank you to Michael Keating, Jürg Steiner, and Robert Young.

N.V.
Toronto, November 2011

Abbreviations

CSF	Community Support Framework
EAGG-F	European Agricultural Guidance and Guarantee Fund
EC	European Community
ERDF	European Regional Development Fund
ESF	European Social Fund
EU	European Union
IMP	Integrated Mediterranean Programs
KEPE	Centre for Planning and Research
KKE	Greek Communist Party
MOU	Management Organization Unit
ND	New Democracy
OP	Operational Programs
OTA	Organization of First-Tier Governments
PASOK	Pan-Hellenic Socialist Movement
PEP	*Perifereiaka Epichirisiaka Programmata* (Regional Operational Programs)
ROP	Regional Operational Programs
SEA	Single European Act
TEDK	Association of Local Authorities
YPETHO/MNE	Ministry of National Economy

EUROPEANIZING GREECE:
THE EFFECTS OF TEN YEARS
OF EU STRUCTURAL FUNDS, 1989–1999

1 Europeanization in the Case of Greece

This book examines the changes that European Union (EU) structural policy made to the Greek administrative and political system in the span of two structural periods: Community Support Framework (CSF) 1989–93 and CSF 1994–9. Although much has been written on member states of the EU and their regions, Greece has not received comparable attention from the academic community.[1] This work makes a modest attempt to fill a void in the literature on the EU and on structural policy in particular. On paper, significant changes have taken place in Greece in a relatively short period of time. There is agreement among academics that Greek politics has been affected by EU membership, but the exact point of Europeanization is a matter of contention. Ioakimidis (1996b), and later Andrikopoulou and Kafkalas (2004), argues that the European Community did not play a role in the introduction of the *perifereia* (region) in Greece, citing a lack of reference to Europe in the legislation. Similarly, Featherstone and Yannopoulos (1995) stress that the structural policy of the mid-1980s – the Integrated Mediterranean Programs (IMPs) – did not seriously challenge the Greek centralist tradition. Alternatively, it can be argued that both the IMPs and CSF (1989–93) were catalysts for the creation of sub-national institutions. Problems encountered with the Community programs provided the impetus for Greek decentralization as it is portrayed in Law 1622/1986. However, this reform was very basic, providing structures with limited personnel. There was also a time lag of eight years (1986–94) during which no significant reforms were introduced. So there was a discrepancy between Greek support of EU membership and a corresponding lethargic record of reform.

The argument made here is that the Greek system was so flawed that it required additional time for the effect to take place. Administrative problems and over-centralization had to be experienced so that the political elites could come to appreciate the shortcomings of the Greek system. Time was also needed for a learning process to take effect on the political actors. This book will show that, unless there is internal acceptance that a system is flawed, there is little possibility of comprehensive change. To change on one's own accord is one thing, but to be told to change is quite another.

Europeanization

The term *Europeanization* has been widely adopted in the discourse of European specialists, despite the fact that there is no consensus on what it is and what it entails.[2] While the concept is related to integration, in that integration leads to the formulation of policies, it is not synonymous with European integration. European integration examines EU development, so researchers debate whether the EU is intergovernmental, neo-functional, supranational, multi-level, or network based. Europeanization generally considers the impact on member states and the national adjustment to the European Union; debates on Europeanization centre on which factors best explain policy or institutional reform. Ladrech defines it as 'a process reorienting the direction and shape of politics to the degree that EC political and economic dynamics become part of the organizational logic of national politics and policy-making' (1994, 69).

Minimally, Europeanization involves a response to the policies of the European Union (Featherstone 2003). This response is dependent upon the fit between the EU policy and the domestic context and the domestic response. Börzel and Risse (2003) argue that there are two conditions for expecting domestic changes in response to Europeanization. First, Europeanization must be 'inconvenient'; in other words, there must be some 'degree of misfit' (Cowles, Caporaso, and Risse 2001; Featherstone and Radaelli 2003; Héritier 2001). Research considers the 'goodness of fit' between European-level processes, policies, and institutions on the one hand, and domestic-level processes, policies, and institutions on the other (Börzel and Risse). This misfit can be in policy, institutions, or both. The worse the fit, the greater the need for a transformation in national policies (Schmidt and Radaelli 2004). There is also the question of policy pressure. Since EU policies have different rules for compliance, they exert different degrees of institutional pressure for change on member states (Schmidt 2002a; Schmidt and Radaelli). If the EU policy poses only a limited difficulty in the intrusiveness of the regulation or in the goodness of fit, 'analysis in terms of learning is not very useful, since absorption of the EU policy is the natural outcome, and "simple learning" the only reasonable response' (Schmidt and Radaelli, 5). Studies using the language of goodness of fit language (Cowles, Caporaso, and Risse 2001; Paraskevopoulos and Leonardi 2004; Risse, Cowles, and Caparaso 2001) examine the level of adaptational pressures that domestic institutions will face in order to comply with the European rules and regulations.

The second criterion for domestic changes in response to Europeanization is that the 'facilitating factors' (actors, institutions, etc.) must respond to adaptational pressures, thus inducing change (Börzel and Risse 2003, 58). These facilitating factors can be viewed as 'intervening factors' (63). Europeanization becomes 'a matter of degree' (Featherstone 2003, 1). The 'goodness of fit' approach conceptualizes learning as a crucial intervening variable between Europeanization and domestic policy / institutional change. The degree of response may involve learning, which, depending on the 'goodness of fit,' may be simple or complicated. A distinction can be made between 'absorption' or simple institutional learning (which is limited to coping mechanisms) and 'transformation' or, in international relations language, 'thick' learning, which leads to doutoro learning and results in institutional development (Bateson 1973; Laird 1999).

Finally, it is also useful to conceptualize the fit–misfit along a continuum, with the point farthest left representing a misfit and the point farthest right – if in fact such a scenario does exist – representing a perfect fit.

All of this is to say that Europeanization has prerequisites. The policy must be intrusive and encompassing, placing expectations on the member state regarding structure and process. The policy must be in contrast to the domestic setting, that is, the structures and processes will not be on par with member state practices. And there must be a domestic response, whereby actors must react to the adaptational pressures, thus inducing change (Börzel and Risse 2003; Vamvakas 2002). Balme and Jouve (1996) outline three scenarios of response: consolidation, superposition, and substitution. Under consolidation, the process could use and reinforce existing networks that handle territorial issues, without any break in national policy procedures. Superposition entails the creation of new, separate networks, without significant impact upon the national policy process – there is simply the addition of a European stratum to public administration. Under substitution, new networks could profoundly alter the whole system and make the existing system obsolete (Balme and Jouve).

Europeanization and EU Structural Policy

Satisfying the First Prerequisite

Regional policy acquired Europeanization potential in the 1989–93 programming period, when it was transformed into a 'meta-policy' with a dual objective: actual funding and – more importantly – process (Hooghe 1996c).[3] The 1988 reforms doubled the funding allocated to structural policy over the 1989–93 period. Further, the European Council adopted regulations enhancing policy evaluation procedures and the decentralization of planning and monitoring authorities. These reforms[4] marked a shift towards a new type of politics grounded in a new development model and new regionalism.[5] The old development approach of the Keynesian school redistributed income to stimulate less-favoured regions. The aim was to shield the region from the negative effects of the market, and the region's role was to shield local producers from the effects of market competition (Nanetti 1996). This top-down approach was applied universally to all types of regions. However, new development emphasized a politics that is complex, diverse, and beyond the boundaries of the nation state; authority is dispersed; and sovereignty is shared under the new development model. It stresses endogenous capacity, human capital training, research and innovation, and the stimulation of networks. Emphasis is placed on institutional cooperation between levels of government and on networking between public and private entities.

While there is no direct connection, this new development theory uses language similar to that used in regime theory. Stone (1989a, 1989b) introduced the notion of a regime in the American context, defined as a constellation of public and private actors who make policy. Regimes are informal, relatively stable coalitions with access to institutional resources that enable them to have a sustained role in making governing decisions. There is a connection here to earlier policy analysis that looks at communities and networks. Regime theory also has antecedents in machine politics and neo-elitist notions of 'mobilization of bias.'

However, the regime school goes further. A regime is a network of elected officials, business elites, and other groups who realize their mutual dependency and seek to cooperate and reach consensus. Although regime theory borrows from the economic paradigm by stressing the importance of business to the community, local politicians are not at the mercy of capital. Rather, they broker the creation of a governing coalition. Politics plays an important role here. In order to be effective, governments realize that they must blend their capacities with those of non-governmental actors. Players hold strategically important positions and collectively are able to provide what individually they cannot. This is an intricate exchange, a partnership in which each player exacts linkages from the others. Consequently, the role of government becomes that of mobilizer and coordinator of resources.

Adopting a similar approach, the EU Economic and Social Committee defined *economic development* as 'a process of changing and enriching the economic structures of an area which forms a uniform cultural, social and economic entity' (Economic and Social Committee of the European Communities 1995).[6] Development entails harnessing resources in a way that may not be identifiable by actors from the outside. The key factor is local control of development so that investment becomes a 'local development action' (ibid.). The 'ultimate aim' is not to increase capital and investment, but rather to reduce local reliance on external aid and to harness individuals to pursue shared community objectives, thereby increasing the local community's confidence in its own resources (ibid.). There is movement to region-specific economic development strategies that are designed and implemented at the regional and local levels so that they are more suitable to the local need. This is program-oriented rather than project-oriented, and the stress is on partnership and cooperation that respects the principle of subsidiarity.[7] So the role of the region moves from that of spectator to that of active participant in development. European, sub-national, and national actors become intermeshed in multiple policy networks, often blurring the distinctions between the three levels (Hooghe 1996a). Some decisional powers are shifted down to municipal, local, and regional governments, while others are transferred up to the EU, and some are shifted simultaneously in both directions (Marks 1993). Local, regional, national, and supranational levels become intertwined in complex patterns of mutual dependence (ibid.).

The 1988 reforms also gave the Commission a highly influential role in regional policymaking, in the designation of areas for funding according to EU criteria, and in the implementation of structural funds, given that member states were required to submit national plans and programs for Commission approval. The Commission embraced its role, moulding structural funds into an instrument of Community policy (Hooghe 1996a; Keating and Hooghe 1996), and advocating and supporting regional participation. This is not surprising, given that the regions bring practical experience to the policy process that is needed for the type of development that the policy seeks to achieve (Keating and Hooghe). Further, information for evaluation and monitoring encourages and in some respects necessitates a bottom-up approach to policymaking.

While it is difficult to argue the existence of a single European administrative system, the EU Structural Programs do presume decentralized management structures. The stress is on process, and results are dependent upon a well-functioning administration that embraces the principle of partnership between levels of administration and between public and private actors. Further, institutions are needed to implement and monitor programs, and to evaluate their performance. Member states must have evaluation capacity in the form of monitoring committees. *Epitropes parakolouthisis* (monitoring committees) are involved in defining the content of evaluation reports and establishing a work program for the evaluators. More importantly, monitoring committees analyse and discuss the completed evaluation reports, and where applicable, propose or advise on possible program changes to maximize the efficiency and effectiveness of the structural funds allocated (European Commission 1999a). Finally, the argument can be made that each EU member state has an interest in ensuring that its sub-national civil service is operating effectively and efficiently, as failure to do so would result in inefficient implementation and absorption of funds. This, in turn, would translate into substantial monetary losses for recipient member states.

It is hardly surprising that structural policy began to penetrate member states by directly engaging national, sub-national, and Commission officials (Marks 1996). Central actors of EU member states realized the need to gain legitimacy and information from local actors, and this made partnership more appealing to them (Hooghe 1996a; Marks). There is an incentive to cooperate, because constitutional authority is not enough. There is also a need for information, funds, expertise, legitimacy, and a capacity to organize (Hooghe 1996c). So again there are parallels to regime theory. Further, the ally that regional actors found in the Commission and the new roles offered regions combined to give regional actors a voice in regional policy.

This cooperative approach of structural policy alters centre–periphery relations in member states. In regional policy after the 1989 period, there was pressure for a vertical redistribution of power between central and sub-national levels of government (Dimitrakopoulos and Passas 2004c). Indeed, if one examines the ex-ante and ex-poste situation of member states, one can determine the impact of cohesion policy on the territorial restructuring of member states (Hooghe 1996c). Even if cohesion policy does not affect institutions, it does affect politics (ibid.).

Europeanization therefore challenges established structures and encourages administrative reform and devolution (Paraskevopoulos 2005; Paraskevopoulos and Leonardi 2004). In this context, Europeanization should be interpreted as being synonymous with institution building (Paraskevopoulos and Leonardi). Interactions between structures and actors requires players to adapt their behaviour to address the challenges to their environment (Paraskevopoulos). This often results in learning, which can undermine the stability of relations between the participating actors.

Greece a Case of Misfit

Satisfying the Second Prerequisite: A Case of Misfit

If structural policy fulfils the criteria of Europeanizing properties, then the Greek case offers a perfect example of policy misfit. On the one hand, the argument can be made that using extreme cases is not a rigorous test. On the other hand, using extreme cases and finding resistance to Europeanization shows the importance of the third prerequisite: the role of agency.

In the early 1990s, the Greek polity was described as having a 'maximum national' and a 'minimal subnational apparatus' (Papageorgiou and Verney 1992). The system of administration was large, ill-coordinated, and inefficient. Some have gone so far as to describe it as a 'colossus with feet of clay' (Sotiropoulos 1993). The political system, while problematic, was even more dysfunctional in the case of structural programs, which presume decentralized planning (Featherstone and Yannopoulos 1995; Getimis and Demetropoulou 2004). The integrative, comprehensive approach of structural programs requires a well-functioning administration that can coordinate the melange of public and private actors involved in the policy community. Much of this was foreign to Greece's administration – a fact that made membership a challenge and an opportunity.

Clientelism

Formally, the Greek state is structured along Napoleonic lines, with a centralized administration, a legalistic constitution, and an ordered bureaucracy. Despite this formal structure, however, clientelism permeates Greek politics to such an extent that the system cannot be understood without a proper understanding of the practice of clientelism (Legg 1969; Mouzelis 1990).

There had been a wider form of clientelism for many years in Greece, which can be traced to the pre-modern Greek state. At that time, an individual's well-being was centred on the family. When external assistance was needed, it was obtained through friendship ties leading from the village to the town, or the *koumbaros* (godfather) – a respected person who was often consulted on marriage, employment, and other important family decisions. Clientelism was particularly evident during the period of the Ottoman Empire, when it was common for local notables in Greece to intercede with Turkish authorities on behalf of the villagers. Turkish officials accepted Greek self-government because it reduced administrative costs and was a means of exploiting subjects.

With the end of Turkish rule in 1829, Greek central elites, first under Capodistrias (1828–31), and later under Otho (1833–44), imported the French model in an attempt to modernize[8] the country, to fulfil the *Megali Idea* (Grand Scheme)[9] and to do away with the clientelist system. Capodistrias hoped to change the social system that had evolved during the Ottoman Empire, which was essentially a taxing mechanism and administrative organization of the enslaved Greeks. The assumption was that an impartial administration would make the patron–client tie unnecessary. In order to establish this kind of administration, the government filled both central and local institutions with individuals who had no personal ties to the local power structure (Legg 1969). This structural change disrupted the dynamics of local communities, wrestling control from the political and social classes of the local notables, and subjecting communities to the institutional administration of the country. This kind of centralization may have been necessary for a country devastated by a war of independence, but it meant destroying the indigenous local communities that existed during the Ottoman period as a peculiar form of decentralized government (Ioakimidis 1996b).[10]

In the end, these attempts to curb the power of local oligarchs led to the assassination of Capodistrias in 1831, at which point Britain, France, and Russia intervened to secure Greece's sovereignty. In his place, the three powers appointed Otho, Prince of Bavaria, as King. Otho immediately set about ruling by absolute methods, confident that institutional changes would undermine local oligarchs by shifting the loyalty of the peasants towards the centre. A royal decree in April 1833 established ten *nomoi* (prefectures) and established *demoi* (municipalities), which replaced the *koinotities* (communities) and subjected them to strict centralization.[11] Problems arose, however, because the imported institutions did not suit the context. To begin with, the majority of the population was still locally focused. Individual horizons did not extend beyond the local community. Indeed, individuals in the periphery were aware of neither the kingdom nor the King. Furthermore, local notables were not prepared to sacrifice their local power bases for the greater cause. While they viewed the King as a necessary evil for securing the *Megali Idea*, their main concern was that their local power bases were being undermined. A final obstruction to centralization was that central elites made the mistake of assuming that they could break through clientelism, underestimating the extent to which it had become entrenched in Greek society. Since society did not change, institutional attempts to regain control were destined to fail unless the tradition of clientelism was accommodated.[12] Patrons and clients were not easily separated; each faction had its own chain of clients for whom it attempted to find state positions. Clientelist ties were strengthened, undermining the centralizing policies of the state, and the patron–client relationship actually flourished (Legg 1969). Representative institutions modelled on those of Western governments were introduced, but Otho's Bavarian advisors were replaced by the old Greek elite who still operated according to traditional methods.

Clientelism and the Centre–Periphery Nexus

The system of regional and local government, established in 1833, remained relatively stable for the nineteenth and most of the twentieth centuries. With the exception of the left wing, which saw decentralization as a way to gain political power, there was not widespread support for decentralization from either the general public or governments in the first two decades following the civil war of 1946–9 (Ioakimidis 1996b). Conservatives were Western oriented in their foreign policy alignment, in their opposition to communism and socialism, and in their support of capitalism. They were not, however, purely modernist, as they supported traditional and authoritarian values. Rational inquiry and fundamental freedoms were associated with the Communist party, with rebellion, and with the rejection of established hierarchy (Fatouros 1993). Indeed, the policy of the dominant right-wing party actually discouraged decentralization and strengthened clientelism.

On the one hand, a turbulent internal and external environment did not encourage decentralist politics from central elites. The experience of the civil war had left a considerable percentage of the population radicalized by a communist-dominated resistance to the Second World War. Despite its military defeat in 1949, the communist-dominated left remained the third force, and in 1958, it emerged as the official opposition. So a fear of a communist uprising made successive governments suspicious of anything involving popular participation, and they kept local government, which was a local bastion for the left wing, as weak as possible. Further, the Macedonian question and the Turkish threat encouraged centralist policies, because a weakening of the centre–periphery nexus was considered a threat to the long-term integrity of the country. On the other hand, Conservative governments attempted to maintain tight control of the state by using patronage as a form of social control. They offered social security in the form of bureaucratic appointment to those who conformed and were deemed politically fit (Verney and Papageorgiou 1992). In effect, the persistence of clientelism allowed individuals and groups to satisfy personal interests through the patron–client tie rather than seek to establish new channels for securing collective goods and services (Verney 1994).

Attempts at even administrative decentralization were modest and were focused on the prefectures. The lower level, comprising almost six thousand units, was, until 1994, the only elected tier of sub-national government. Members of municipal and local councils were directly elected by universal suffrage and secret ballot. Local authorities had power in local affairs, provided that these did not conflict with the Constitution or other legislation. This included responsibility for water supply, drainage, roads, public squares, bridges, parks, sport facilities, markets, kindergartens, urban transport, parking, and pasture lands. They could also provide amenities for tourists, low-cost housing, social services, and health facilities, and could create industrial and commercial firms and restore historic buildings. Local councils drew up their local budget, established policy on matters falling within their competence, and decided on the local tax rates, duties,. and dues.[13] However, all decisions of local governments had to have the approval of the prefect. This provided the centre with control by allowing the prefect the power to delay implementation.

In 1955, Law 3200 allocated prefectures a separate public works budget, and set up a prefecture fund to handle it. *Nomarchiaka symboulia* (prefectoral councils) were established to discuss prefecture public works programs, to make proposals concerning the development of the prefecture, and to consider the functioning of public services and matters involving health and welfare. However, councils served only an advisory function; they met twice each year and were made up of central civil servants and local government officials. Further, the fact that councils were headed by a *nomarchis* (prefect), appointed by the minister of the interior, who was in charge of the decentralized services of the central ministries located in the prefectures, meant that they posed no threat to centralization. In effect, prefectures continued to function as de-concentrated units of central government.

Having said this, centralization, a prefectoral system, and a clientelist culture can become mutually reinforcing and produce complicated power relations at sub-national levels. Over time, clientelism can also be 'reinterpreted' and 'updated' (Piattoni 1997) so that the relationship can be conceived as essentially personalized, affected, and reciprocal, and between actors or sets of actors commanding unequal resources and involving mutually beneficial transactions (Lemarchand and Legg 1972, 51–2).

In its traditional guise, clientelism can be traced and explained in terms of a 'godfather' or 'kinship' tie (Gilsenan 1977; Legg 1969; Weingrod 1977), which is based on personal loyalty, obligation, and the exchange of unequal goods and services (Lemarchand and Legg 1972). The gains are individualistic and atomistic rather than collective. The tie offers status to the patron and security to the client. The relationship is between unequals, combining inequality and interdependence, but the client is not a pawn in a one-way relationship (Médard 1981; Scott 1977a). Indeed, if the patron could perform the task without the client, he would have no reason to establish the tie. In some cases, clientelism is only a transitional device or a means of coping with the clash between tradition and modernization. As modern institutions are introduced, technocratic elites may penetrate the system and change the role of the patron. In other cases, such as Greece, clientelism persists and begins to serve new functions and expands, often losing its dyadic, one-to-one quality to include clusters and networks of actors (Scott 1977b).

As old forms of clientelism disappear, new ones emerge to take their place or function alongside more established forms (Zuckerman 1977). On the one hand, clientelism is an attempt of the centre elite to maintain control over the periphery. Since regional representatives are central appointees, clientelism can curb sub-national mobilization. On the other hand, since the locus of decision-making is at the centre, there is a need for local politicians to find a mediator, which can be satisfied through the patron–client tie. From a structuralist perspective, clientelism can be a response to the institutional dependence of sub-national levels of government on the political administrative system (Médard 1981). That is, the decision-making apparatus at the centre reinforces the dependency in which the prefect and local notables are both patrons and clients (Médard). Although there is no question of equality or inequality, the dyadic relationship between the prefect and local notable is asymmetrical, because local notables compete for favours from the prefect, but the reverse is not actually true (Médard). The local politician, however, need not bow to officials from the centre because the latter control the resources. Nor is the political administration necessarily an obstacle for local elites, because they may utilize it for their own benefit. In the French case, for example, there is a complexity in the political administrative system, which is not easily identified.[14] Grémion (1976) argues that local notables build a *pouvoir périphérique* that has a form of power, having both an internal and external dimension. The internal dimension is based at the local level and involves the relationship between the notable and the local community; the external dimension is based on links between the notable and the central bureaucracy and its peripheral ramifications. So the prefect mediates between the centre and the local level, and the local notable mediates between the central administration and the citizen. Hence, there is not a one-way relationship in which the centre controls the periphery, but rather a mutual dependence. Under such conditions, clientelism 'must be viewed as a persistently pragmatic response to a system in which centralization and dependency have become self-perpetuating phenomena' (Médard, 169).

Clientelism and the System of Administration

While it was common in other democratic countries for the incoming party to change personnel and bureaucratic structures, in Greece, a change in government resembled a change of regime. In contrast to other EU member states where the politicians were amateurs compared to their bureaucrats, the situation in Greece was reversed. Clientelism became the method of bureaucratic appointment, with civil servant positions often secured through one's *meson* (connections).[15] Members of parliament were considered the 'kings of *rousfeti*' (political favours) because they determined positions and displaced civil servants. This custom of bureaucratic clientelism 'consists of a systemic infiltration of the state machine by party devotees and the allocation of favours through it … Such a party becomes a collective patron … The public bureaucracy is oriented less towards the effective performance of public service than towards the provision of parasitic jobs for the political clientele of the ruling sectors, in exchange for their political support' (Lyrintzis 1984, 103–4).

There exists what Sotiropoulous (2004) terms 'clientelism at the top' and 'clientelism at the bottom.' The former involves political appointment in the upper echelons of the ministries – a practice that is not distinct to Greece. In the United States, for example, close to ten thousand positions change hands with every change in president. Given the large size of the American administration, this figure is not substantial. Equivalent numbers in a comparatively smaller administration such as Greece's create a more exaggerated practice (Sotiropoulos). Clientelism at the bottom – party patronage – creates problems in that civil servants often lack the skills needed for planning and financing. Hence, it became necessary for each incoming party to hire political appointees with the skills necessary to manage the state (Sotiropoulos 1993). Technical skill was found in political parties, but it was lacking in the bureaucracy. In addition, the high turnover of personnel meant that there was a lack of permanency, and of skill that otherwise would have been acquired through experience. Finally, clientelism increased the size of the public sector, but the result was not better service to the citizen. On the one hand, there was an uneven distribution of personnel on account of the erratic application of the clientelist criteria when planning human resources, which meant that some areas such as Athens were overstaffed while others were lacking in personnel (Sotiropoulos 2004). On the other hand, from a behavioural perspective, the bureaucracy was plagued with corruption and inefficiency. Civil servants operated in a clientelist manner; they were not impartial when performing their duties and often required boosts in the form of *fakelakia* (side-payments) to perform their tasks. Legal rules combined with a poorly trained, inexperienced bureaucracy and a clientelist culture to create a bureaucratic backlog.

· However, an illusion of reform was maintained. With every change in government there followed the passage of new administrative legislation (Sotiropoulos 1993; Spanou 1995). Indeed, between 1951 and 1981, clientelism was abolished on paper numerous times. Legislation attempted to provide some uniformity and order to the anarchic political-clientelist situation. It outlined uniform rules for the status of civil servants and established selection and recruitment procedures based on merit. But Greece failed to achieve Western standards. Clientelism breeds an inflation of legislation and regulations (Sotiropoulos 2004). The problem was that laws and decrees were not considered rules to be respected, but only obstacles to be circumvented (Sotiropoulos 1993; Spanou; Tsoukalas 1987). In order to combat clientelism, there had to be a change in society and in ways of thinking. Since both patrons and clients benefited, pressures from below met with willingness of those in power to satisfy tradition at the expense of the objectives of reform (Spanou). The governing party benefited because the bureaucracy did not conflict with the party, but it was part of the political game, acting as an annex to it. Civil servants benefited from the employment and from the side-payments they received from citizens wishing to expedite the administrative process. Consequently, at no point were the political personnel and the advantages of clientelism seriously questioned.

Europeanization and the Role of Agency

Satisfying the Third Prerequisite

Two pieces of evidence demonstrate the presence of Europeanizing forces in Greece in the 1990s. The first is the comprehensive legislative reforms instituted in the decade; the second is that the *nomimotis* (legal state) approximates the *pragmatikotis* (real state). In other words, reforms were not empty shells. The normative test seeks to understand the logic behind the reforms and the results. Although there was decentralization in the formal sense, in practice, central elites could have tried to find ways around it. The goal here is to identify the components that Greek politicians were trying to incorporate into their reforms. This means identifying changes in structure (decentralization), personnel (the placement of qualified civil servants), and the way the administration functions. The last component includes finer elements such as communication. This is more than language. Civil servants and politicians must be able to communicate their needs and positions to their

European counterparts and understand their European counterparts' positions, needs, behaviour, and reactions, and to find acceptable solutions for all parties involved (Leitner 2000).

Considering the past failures at reform, it was key to establish how politics was being played and how the system was functioning. The empirical test undertaken in this book examines policymaking, implementation, and performance in the Integrated Mediterranean Programs, and in the First (1989–93) and Second (1994–9) Structural Programming periods. The assumption is that if the administrative structures are in place, and if the political system is decentralized, there will be a quantitative and qualitative improvement in performance. I use data from interviews at the national, sub-national, and EU levels to detect these finer changes. Examining the relationship between actors at the centre and periphery and the relationship between the *perifereia* and the prefectures helped to establish whether there was a change in the ideologies of the players and whether there were new ways of thinking at both national and sub-national levels. For real reform, there must be two sets of Europeanizing elites: one at the centre, so that the legislation is passed and there is a real devolution of power to the periphery; the other in the periphery, because these are the individuals who are given the devolved powers. There must also be a qualitative improvement in centre–periphery relations. So there are both qualitative and quantitative indicators of Europeanization (Méndez, Wishlade, and Yuill 2007). A qualitative understanding of the dynamics of policy and context can be seen as a complement to quantitative approaches, and 'policy researchers ignore this at their peril' (ibid., 17). Indeed the very nature of the phenomenon of clientelism makes research with solid data a very difficult task. The qualitative approach is more fitting to the complexity of the topic.

Variation among the political elites, despite the fact that the majority of them supported EU membership, was expected. The old elite is traditionalist in its outlook and unenthusiastic about Europe, trying to keep the political system as it was: centralized and clientelist. A modernizing elite has an interest in Europe and experience in policymaking in Brussels – a group much more open to new ways of thinking. The Pan-Hellenic Socialist Movement (PASOK), in power for most of the 1990s, was dominated by a pro-European elite, who were interested in modernizing the Greek political system, because they saw that in order to take full advantage of membership of the EU, they had to enact real reforms.

A decentralized Greek system could involve a reconfiguration of clientelism in the periphery. Local entrenched interests may oppose change and concentrate on divisive benefits, scattering funds on small projects to win political favour rather than spending on large-scale projects that are part of a broader regional vision. Better-trained civil servants may simply result in a refinement of the practice of clientelism; the additional level of administration may simply create extra layers of corruption. The more layers of government there are, the more civil servants there are with contracts, favours, and *rousfeti* to distribute. The system could absorb Europe and use EU funds to extend the practice of clientelism in such a way that the traditional mode of operation reconfigured across multiple levels. Alternately, a new type of political system might emerge – modern and decentralized.

Piattoni (1997) argues that change in the type of clientelism can take place if a system is subject to external shocks, such as if patrons change their strategy, or if the pressure from clients changes.[16] Since clientelism has persisted for centuries in Greece, there must be a strong impetus if it is to change. The hypothesis was that membership in the EU would provide this force because it gave Greek political elites the incentive to change the dynamics of the system. The new elite had an interest in modernization and decentralization, and they had the opportunity to establish a new type of politics that was not based on clientelism, at least not a clientelism that worked against development.

The working hypothesis of the book was that the reformed structure and changed politics would alter clientelism: it would disappear as a method of bureaucratic appointment, but it would remain, at least in the short run, as a method of interaction between actors of policy communities. Patron–client ties can be used to different ends, so the role of agency is important here. It was expected that with decentralization would come an empowerment of peripheral actors that would convert them into partners. This new form of elite cooperation would resemble a Mediterranean regime. As noted above, the complexity and interdependence of EU structural policy is in line with Stone's concept of regime. There is, however, a question of context. Stone admits that his notion of regime, while applicable to American politics, may not apply elsewhere. This raises particular concerns when analysing politics in Europe. In the latter case, it may be suitable to consider the concept of a Mediterranean regime, which, as the label suggests, entails an interaction based on mutual need. The notion of cooperation and mutual benefit is very much in line with the premise behind EU policymaking and implementation. With EU interaction, actors adopt some of the EU characteristics and processes. The theoretical framework here is the multi-level approach to the European Union. This approach means that sovereignty in the European Union is divided among the European, national, and regional levels.

Tsarouhas (2008) argues that Europeanization entails the potential imitation of successful policy paradigms. In the case of Greece, the regime may exhibit elements of clientelism; so it helpful to distinguish it as a Mediterranean regime. I make the assumption that there is a culture with its own distinctive characteristics that can be labelled Mediterranean; that in the context of politics, this interaction involves personalistic, informal, ad hoc modes of operation; and that this interaction resembles a regime in that actors come together to secure collectively what they could not secure individually. Here clientelism need not be an obstacle to development or even to the general functioning of a political system. The informal nature of clientelism helps smooth relations among different levels of administration and government in Greece. Clientelism is the glue that binds the centre to the periphery; it facilitates the system of distribution and redistribution; and it enables interaction between actors across multiple levels.

Fieldwork

The use of over seventy semi-structured interviews[17] with high-level policymakers and political actors helped determine the extent to which central actors perceived a need for real change and the extent to which sub-national actors gained a voice. The bulk of the interviews took place between 1999 and 2001. They were semi-structured in that a questionnaire was not given. Instead, general questions were asked, such as the interviewee's position on EU membership. As the interview progressed and the interviewee became more comfortable, the more difficult questions such as the practice of clientelism and relations with other key actors were asked.

Officials at the sub-national, national, and EU levels were interviewed to obtain the widest possible sample to cross-check findings. At the centre, officials in the Ministry of the Interior were interviewed to establish the type of devolution that the PASOK government intended to implement. Interviews were also held with officials in the Ministry of the National Economy to obtain an understanding of how structural policy was being implemented. From the periphery, interviews with the *nomarches* (prefects) of Achaia and Thessaloniki and the *perifereiarchi* (regional secretary) of West Greece were conducted in order to obtain a better understanding of the regional elite and the form and strength of sub-national mobilization. At the EU level, officials in the Regional Policy Directorate-General of the European Commission, and the directorates responsible for Greece were interviewed because they offered a valuable 'external' opinion on the performance and politics of Greece.

Interviews provided a substantial amount of the hard data required for this study. Quantitative data found within documents and reports from the *perifereies* and from the European Commission were essential to track implementation of EU policy and to further test my hypotheses. Officials in the EU Commission (DG XVI) were well organized and able to access necessary data easily. In Greece, there was some difficulty in obtaining data on implementation, because sometimes there was some confusion among civil servants about what level of administration had what data.

The case studies presented below involve the regions of West Greece and Central Macedonia and their respective capital city prefectures: the Prefecture of Thessaloniki in Central Macedonia, and the Prefecture of Achaia in West Greece. These areas were selected because their geographical locations and metropolitan centres were equally important.[18] It seemed to me that, if sub-national elites were to be mobilized to advance regional interests, these were ideal places to start.

Structure of the Book

The book focuses on the region, primarily because of its direct connection to EU structural funds and the uniqueness of the situation, given that the regional tier was non-existent prior to the EU programs. Furthermore, the third tier has the strongest connection to Europeanization, and its absence translated in the greatest misfit. While the relationship of the first tier to the other two sub-national levels is touched upon throughout the book, this work does not offer a systematic breakdown of the reforms as they pertain to the first tier.

Chapter 2 examines reforms in two periods: 1981–93 and 1994–9. The former period is a pseudo attempt to address the shortcomings of the system; it appears that neither EU membership in general, nor the IMPs and CSF (1989–93), provided sufficient force to effect significant change. The post-1994 period, however, was a different matter; it was during this period that comprehensive changes were introduced. Chapters 3 and 4 present case studies, which attempt to show how the Greek administrative model operates in practice by subjecting it to two tests. Chapter 3 provides an empirical test by examining policymaking, implementation, and performance in the integrated Mediterranean programs, and in the first (1989–93) and second (1994–9) structural development periods. Devolution and partnership are therefore considered in the context of EU structural policymaking and implementation. Findings suggest a strong connection between decentralization and European integration in general, and the structural funds in particular. The tentative conclusion, based on Greece's performance in the EU programs, is that the administration and the centre–periphery nexus were improving, and that clientelism was slowly changing for the better. Chapter 4 provides a normative test and outlines the findings generated from the interviews of central, sub-national, and Commission officials. Here the logic behind the reforms and the results is presented, along with an assessment of the role of agency. The reasons behind the introduction of the reforms played a key role in determining whether the reforms succeeded or failed. The aim was to determine the extent to which central actors perceived a need for real change and the extent to which ideas of decentralization were becoming entrenched in Greek politics. Further, it was important to establish the extent to which sub-national actors were gaining a voice and adopting different levels of cooperation so that they could take advantage of new opportunities to effect real change. Approaching Europeanization from the bottom up, it is argued that some aspects were unintended by the central actors. Finally, chapter 5 offers a summary of the findings and speculation about the future, in conjunction with material from interviews of upper-level civil servants and political figures.

The main argument here is that although much still depends on how the elites mediate the adjustment, the internal system has been disturbed. Indeed, relationships between actors in policy networks related to the EU structural funds were found to exhibit at least some of the characteristics of a Mediterranean regime. Returning to the language of Balme and Jouve (1996) and the question of consolidation, superposition, or substitution, the conclusion here is that the Greek case falls somewhere between superposition and substitution.

2 Europeanization Manifested in Legislative Reforms

Andrikopoulou and Kafkalas (2004, 45–6) argue that Greece underwent four stages towards EU membership that mirrored its stance on regional policy and determined its Europeanization. The period between 1981 and 1985 can be described as a passive intergovernmental or defensive mode, where the dominant stance emphasized pride in the homogenizing supranational EC structures (45). Between 1986 and 1990, Greek officials pursued an active intergovernmental or offensive mode. This second stage witnessed the introduction of the IMPs and the reforms for CSF (1989–93). During the supranational passive or inactive mode (1991–5), Greece was trying to regain its credibility from the rest of the EU. During 1996–2000, in the supranational active or cooperative mode, there was an understanding among Greek officials that securing gains from membership should be the result of only a more responsible attitude (46).

The first two stages fall under the Euro-sceptic umbrella. If actors are Euro-sceptic, Europeanization cannot be expected. Further, if actors are Euro-sceptic, any external claims about the shortcomings of the domestic system will not be accepted. The 1990s witnessed the emergence of Euro-philic Greek actors and hence the expectation of Europeanizing effects. This chapter examines reforms and attempts at reform of the Greek political system. It shows that Greek support for EU membership was insufficient incentive to induce change. It also shows that initially, pressure of the reformed structural funds was also not enough. It concludes that time is key, in that it allows actors to realize the need for change and perhaps decide to act.

Membership of the EU: Pseudo-Europeanization

With the fall of the Junta in 1974, the Greek government under the leadership of Karamanlis sought to democratize and modernize the political system. In 1975, a new constitution re-established a parliamentary system that was more democratic than those in the past. Political elites looked to the French system once again and modelled the Greek state after the French Fifth Republic.[1] This time, however, they sought something deeper than simply copying Western Europe. The right-wing political elite wanted to actually become a part of Western Europe.

The main pro-Europe party in Greece was Karamanlis's New Democracy Party.[2] Karamanlis played a major role in convincing the Council of Ministers to bypass the Commission's suggestions that Greece wait until her economic and political situation was consolidated. For Greeks in favour of accession and for Karamanlis in particular, the EC promised both political and economic benefits. Membership was considered the best way to escape Greece's dependency on external assistance for financial and foreign policy objectives, and was expected to entrench the restored democracy and secure fundamental freedoms, majority rule, and the rule of law (Fatouros 1993; Ioakimidis 1993; Kazakos 1994). There were, however, few political reforms in the years leading up to EC membership and immediately after Greece's accession.

Decentralization

The 1975 Constitution provided for the creation of new levels of government, but the structures of local government did not change. The same can be said of PASOK, which came to power in 1981 with a commitment to decentralize (Paraskevopoulos 2005). Although not related to Europe, its manifesto promised to establish new tiers of local government at secondary and tertiary levels. The reforms of Law 1235/1982, however, were very modest. The prefectoral councils were to be a first step towards creation of new tiers of local government. This was in no way an administrative attempt to rationalize an overly centralized system, and political devolution was not considered. Councils were still primarily advisory, and since most of the bodies in the councils were dominated by the governing party, there was little chance that they would challenge central power (Verney 1994). Finally, the legislation reinforced the dependency of the prefect by allowing the government to dismiss and appoint prefects at will.[3]

The next attempt at decentralization was linked to Community structural funding. In 1985, Greece was divided into six geographic areas: the Aegean Islands, Attica, Central and Eastern Greece, Crete, Northern Greece, and Western Greece / Peloponnese (the seventh Greek IMP dealt with informatics that covered all of Greece). These regions were not given any political institutions or administrative structures. They functioned merely as monitoring committees that addressed the progress of Community funding – the IMPs.

In 1986, reforms addressed decentralization at both second (prefectoral) and third (regional) sub-national levels. Law 1622 provided two means of decentralization: the popular election of prefects and prefectoral councils; and the division of the country into thirteen *perifereies* (regions). To begin, it should be stressed that the prefectoral elections were not directly linked to EU regional policy.[4] The legislation states that approximately three-quarters of the prefectoral councils are to be directly elected for four-year terms, with elections to be held at the same time as municipal elections. The prefectoral council is described as a 'decisive organ of the prefectoral self-administration deciding on *matters falling within its jurisdiction*' (emphasis added). Councils were intended to have responsibility for economic, social, and cultural development in *their assigned area*. Indeed, the legislation clearly states that the relationship between the first and second tiers is not hierarchical. The prefectures are given the responsibility of drawing up the prefecture's medium-term development program. The council is expected to formulate and present to the regional council (see below) proposals for works affecting the prefecture, but which are part of the mid-term regional or national development program. If implemented, the legislation would have altered relationships among tiers of administration. Prefects were to remain as organs of the central administration, but their role was downgraded. They were to face two power sources: one from above (because they could be recalled by the centre at any time) and a strengthened one from below (since prefectoral councils comprised full-time elected officials). Prefects lost control over the agenda, and they no longer presided over council meetings. However, 'the prefect can make null by his/her own direction the acts of all the organs of the prefectoral self-administration which are contrary to the law.'

Part 3 of Law 1622 also established thirteen administrative regions (*perifereies*). The *perifereia* was a new administrative unit that coordinated policy and administration between the centre and the prefectures. The legislation states that the *'perifereies* divide the country for the purpose of planning, programming, and coordinating regional development.' *Perifereies* were the basic unit for the European regional development plans under the Community Support Framework (Papageorgiou and Verney 1992). They corresponded to geographical areas, although only some had pre-existing identities. Article 65 determined that each region would be headed by a *perifereiarchis* (regional secretary) appointed by the central government, who would hold the position of first-degree official (special position). Regional secretaries were the 'direct representatives of the government responsible for the implementation of the government's policy in the region.' For matters of official status, the regional secretary was responsible to the Ministry of the Interior, but on specific matters he or she was accountable to the respective ministry.

Regional councils (*perifereiacho symboulia*) were modelled on prefectoral councils and chaired by the regional secretary. Regional councils comprise the state-appointed prefects of all prefectures of the region, the presidents of the prefectoral self-administrations of these same prefectures, and a representative of the union of local municipalities and communities from each prefecture of the region a person elected along with their replacement from their administrative committee. Provision was also made for new regional level offices and the placement of civil servants in accordance with the division of the country. The councils would be responsible for formulating public-sector proposals and presenting to the centre works and measures concerning the *perifereia*; preparing the semi-annual regional development programs following the specific proposals of the prefectoral councils; and distributing the funding of the programs of public investment for works of prefectoral and local importance.

Elections were not held at the prefectoral level. In actual fact, the legislation as it pertained to the prefectures was not implemented for eight years, at which time a new law was introduced. Regional secretaries were first appointed in 1988. Regional councils followed soon afterwards, but they were formed ad hoc, bringing together central, prefectoral, and Commission officials to monitor the implementation of EU structural funds. Regional secretaries were given only a skeleton staff of administrators recruited from the Offices of the Central Administration (Papageorgiou and Verney 1992). Regions were intended to coordinate planning and to monitor the regional budget. However, the *perifereia* was not given political institutions, administrative structures, or a

working budget and consequently could not properly perform its designated responsibilities (Papageorgiou and Verney). In March 1990, the
'ecumenical' government[5] legislated for elections to be held in October
1990, but when Nea Democratia (New Democracy, or ND) came to
power in April 1990, the elections were promptly called off.

The System of Administration

Attempts to reform the public administration were equally disappointing. In 1981, the PASOK government sought to correct the mal-
administration, the practice of clientelism, and apparent lack of respect
for the civil servant (Spanou 1995). In its first term in office, it legislated
a series of reforms. It established the National Centre for Public Administration and introduced service training programs. Law 1400/1983
addressed the appraisal system and the abolition of civil servants' personal files. Law 1320/1983 changed the recruitment system, introducing a computerized system that calculated objective criteria points for
each candidate. But the problem was that the importance given to the
candidate's 'social profile' meant that qualifications took second place.
In the end, the practice of clientelism worsened, because PASOK came
to power after years of Nea Democratia rule and considered electoral
victory an opportunity to offer rewards to its supporters by giving
them employment in the public sector.

During PASOK's first term, the government placed several hundred
of its own people in top administrative posts, dismissing all top administrative personnel in the ministries and the prefectures. In its
second term in office (1985–9), it introduced another grade system
(Law 1586/1986), addressed the relationship between the citizen and
the administration (Law1599/1986), and changed the recruitment system once again (Law 1735/1987) so that the weight of social criteria was
reduced. These reforms sought to abolish clientelism by introducing
uniform, binding rules, and planning procedures for recruitment
(Spanou 1995). In the end, however, the legislation was not put into
effect (Spanou).

When Nea Democratia returned to power in 1990, it also attempted
to modernize the civil service. It followed a neo-liberal ideology of limited state intervention and privatization and promised to reduce the
size of the public sector. It re-established the post of general directorates
abolished under PASOK (Law 1892/1990), introduced a new grade system (Law 2085/1992), and appointed its supporters to top management

posts. Further, Law 1943/1991 promised modernization and a comprehensive civil service reform on two fronts: it introduced the merit principle, and it introduced new methods and procedures to establish transparency and to improve service to citizens. On paper, then, it abolished clientelism both as a method of bureaucratic appointment and in the functioning of the civil service (relation between citizens and the civil servants). In practice, however, Nea Democratia, like PASOK, hired several hundred of its own people in top administrative posts, dismissing all top administrative personnel in the ministries and the prefectures. Once again, there was no significant change.

Both the ND and PASOK parties have, at different times, enacted laws and decrees to correct the problems plaguing the Greek administration (Sotiropoulos 1993; Spanou 1995). When in power, both parties advocated some version of a rational and neutral administration. However, in the early 1990s, Greece's divergences from other European countries became more explicit (Spanou). The administration was incapable of ensuring continuity and was dominated and controlled by the party in power. Additionally, patronage undermined the technical capacity and legitimacy of the public service. Sotiropoulos argues that these problems were not simply technical or legal. In order to succeed, reform had to combat clientelist traditions in society and in the political system. Despite the apparent intentions of successive administrations, pressure from 'clients' combined with the willingness of those in power to satisfy tradition at the expense of reform.

Evidence of Europeanism: Post-1994 Reforms

In the mid-1990s, administrative reforms gathered momentum, and the pseudo-attempts at decentralization seen throughout the 1980s were finally fleshed out. In 1994, Law 2218 took another look at the prefectures.[6] Article 1 established *nomarchiakes autodoikisis* (prefectoral governments) as the 'second-level organization of local self-government.' Prefectoral council members were to be directly elected by universal and secret ballot every four years at the same time as the municipal elections. The prefect was elected from among candidate prefects of the winning coalition. The number of council members was once again proportional to the population of the prefecture, ranging from twenty-one members for populations of up to one hundred thousand, to thirty-seven for prefectures having a population greater than two hundred thousand. In the first and third year of its term, the prefectoral council elected from among its members the president/chair, the vice-president, and the secretary by an absolute majority of those present. The prefect was not president of the council. Prefectoral governments receive revenues from duties, taxes, entitlements, and contributions; income from the exploitation of property; specific annual economic reinforcement of the tactical budget for covering the costs of administering state responsibilities transferred to prefectoral governments; and central independent resources. Each prefectoral council was to responsible for:

- regulation of the matters of the council, the prefectoral committees, and the organization of the offices of the prefecture;
- implementation of the proceedings of democratic planning;
- the budget and the statement of receipts and disbursement of the NA and legal personnel;
- imposition of duties, taxes, contribution; and entitlements …;
- study, building, and maintenance of works …;
- election of members of the prefectoral committee;
- filling empty positions of civil servants of the prefecture (Article 13).

As was the case with Law 1622, there was no hierarchical relationship between the first and second tiers. The prefect did not vote in the council, but if he or she was absent, the meeting would be invalid. The prefect was the representative of the prefectoral government, carried out the decisions of the prefectoral council, and was responsible for the prefectoral government.

Law 2218 also readdressed the *perifereia*, marking the first significant steps to creating a proper area of regional state administration. Article 49, entitled 'Administrative Division of the State,' reads, 'The *perifereies* into which the country is divided in accordance with Article 61 of Law 1622/1986 for the planning, programming and coordination of the regions' development are also administrative regions and constitute an administrative unit of the state.'

Following Law 1622, the legislation established in every *perifereia* a regional council comprising a regional secretary of the region as chair; the prefects of the region (now directly elected); a representative from every local union of municipalities and communities (TEDK) in the *perifereia*, who is elected along with a representative from the governing committee of the TEDK; one representative for each regional organization such as the Chambers of the Productive Sectors, the Technical

Chambers of Greece, the Geotechnical Chamber of Greece, and the Economic Chamber of Greece. Ministry representatives were permitted to attend meetings but were not allowed to vote.

The regional council was convened with the decision of the general secretary of the region. It was given the powers outlined in Article 63 of Law 1662/1986. Further, in the headquarters of each *perifereia*, there was introduced a *perifereiako tameio anaptixis* (regional development treasury), to be supervised by the minister of the interior.[7] The Treasury was to be an organ of programming and development and to act in accordance with the decisions of the regional council. It undertook all programming measures of the *perifereia* within the framework of European development. So, unlike Law 1622, there was reference to the EU. The legislation states that the Treasury is responsible for:

- administration, funding coming from the programs of the EU;
- distribution of the above funds to the administrative authorities of the programs, in accordance with the decisions of the regional council;
- imposition, confirmation, and collection of taxes/duties, entitlements, and collections towards the Treasury following the approval of the regional council;
- the participation in programs of the EU …;
- the reinforcement, and technical support so that *perifereies* can perform their functions, particularly regional development programs (Article 53).

Under the new system, the regional secretary is president of the Treasury. He or she represents the Treasury in courts, carries out the decisions of the Treasury, and orders the collection of funds for the Treasury. The Treasury, in turn, is administered by an administrative council, which is put together by the regional secretary for a four-year term. Its members include the regional secretary as chair, a representative of the first-tier government, a representative of the second-tier governments, a representative from the employer organizations, a representative from labour organizations, and two supervisors of the *perifereia* who are appointed by the regional secretary. Among the resources of the Regional Treasury is a percentage of the financing it administers, determined by the Ministry of the National Economy (MNE) and the Ministry of the Interior; revenues from the imposition of taxes and duties; and revenues from participation in programs instituted by the

European Union. Provision is also made to staff the Treasury with qualified, trained professionals. Also, mention is made of EU programs and the need for technical support.

The position of the regional secretary was modelled on that of the prefect in the pre-1994 period, although the former had fewer powers. The regional secretary fulfilled a supervisory function. Article 18 states that 'all acts of the prefectoral council, the prefectoral committee, and the administrative councillors are forwarded to the general secretary of the region within five days of the meeting along with a copy of the certificate of publication.' Within five days of receiving the act, the regional secretary had to send decisions/acts that he or she considered illegal (along with explanation) to a tri-member committee. This committee was established in every prefecture and comprised:

- one judge of a court of justice as chair appointed, along with his or her replacement, by the chair of the judges of the court of justice;
- one upper-level civil servant of the Ministry of the Interior, and in the event that was no other ministry, the NPDD [Legal Persons of Dimosion Dikaiou], who is appointed along with his replacement by the general secretary of the Region;
- one member of the prefectoral council appointed along with his or her representative by the prefectoral council (Article 18).

The committee belongs to the Ministry of the Interior. It is convened at the request of the regional secretary and by the invitation of the chair 'to examine the legality of the acts of the prefectoral council, prefectoral committee ... which are referred to the committee by the general secretary of the region.' Reference is again made to the EU, where the law states that 'when the NA carries out its responsibilities for the enforcement of legislation of the European Union, it is subject to the inspection that legislation provides.' Further, in matters involving the treasury of the prefecture, such as the collection of revenue, the prefectoral authorities must provide any information that the regional secretary requests. If it is found that the prefect and members of the prefectoral council have committed a serious violation of their duties, or have exceeded their powers because of fraud or serious oversight, the regional secretary can impose the administrative sanction of suspension and allowance of up to three months. This responsibility was given to the centrally appointed prefect under legislation 1622. In effect, the general secretary of the region is a transferable employee belonging to the category of special posts, who holds a grade 1 post and is appointed, dismissed, and transferred from region to region by act of the cabinet, which is issued after recommendation by the minister of the interior. He or she directs, coordinates, oversees, and controls the activities of the services and employees of the region. The responsibilities assigned or transferred to the services of the region are the exclusive competency of the general secretary.[8]

In 1997, two more significant pieces of legislation were introduced: Laws 2539 and 2503. Law 2539/1997 (part of the Capodistrias Plan) reduced the number of local tiers from 5,823 to 1,033 (municipalities increased from 441 to 900, while communities decreased from 5,382 to 133). Here, it was acknowledged that reforms at the prefectoral and regional levels were necessary to bring Greece into the twenty-first century (Prologue of Law 2539/1997; interviews Ministry of the Interior). In chapter 4, we will see how these reductions created stronger local actors and changed the relations among sub-national tiers.

Whereas Law 2218 addressed both the prefectures and the *perifereies*, Law 2503 focused on the *perifereies* only. It transforms the region into a devolved administrative entity with its own organization, budget, and staff. Article 2 provides for the transfer of personnel of the ministries that placed directorates in the region. Provision was also made to staff the regional administration with qualified personnel. Article 8 distinguished between permanent civil servants and personnel hired for an unspecified period. Permanent civil servants were divided into four categories: A–university trained, B–technological trained, C–second-level trained, and D–mandatory trained. Emphasis was placed on Category A servants, and legislation encouraged the placement of experts in the *perifereies* – specialists such as economists, civil engineers, geotechnicians, biologists, environmentalists, regional development specialists, and so on. The hiring of non-permanent officials in particular, was also necessary in order to ensure the proper management of Programs of European Social Funds, European Regional Development Funds, and European Agricultural Funds. These individuals could be categorized as specialists, technical personnel with secondary training, or assistants with mandatory training. In an attempt to encourage the movement of civil servants, they were guaranteed the same benefits as their counterparts in the central ministries.

The two main instruments of the *perifereies* are the Office of the Regional Secretary and the General Directorates of the *Perifereia*. The General Directorate is composed of all the directorates and the independent sectors and offices of those regions with seats within its administrative limits. The directorates are:

- Planning and Development
- Health and Welfare
- Public Works
- Monitoring of Construction of Work
- Monitoring of Maintenance of Work
- Environment and Planning
- Forests
- Agricultural Development
- Self-Administration
- Administration by the self-contained sectors: the Department of Communications and Assistance of Citizens and the Office of Policy Protection (Article 5).

Directorates are divided into departments and have local powers and responsibility for all the *perifereia*. They are responsible for carrying out studies, and for organizing, programming, supervising, and monitoring policy implementation. To use the Directorate of Planning and Development as an example, it is responsible for implementing regional policy at the level of the *perifereia*, and for instituting annual and semi-annual programs of regional development. This directorate is subdivided into four departments: Motivation of Regional Development, Management of Water Resources, Regional Policy Planning, and Program Implementation and Project Management. A director general must have a university degree and at least fifteen years of state service. Those selected by the Ministry of the Interior are placed by the decision of the regional secretary for three years. The director general works with the regional secretary to plan the policies of the region and works with the offices of the central administration to ensure that national policies and the policies of the *perifereia* are properly implemented. He or she coordinates the activity of all offices of the region, ensuring communication and harmonious cooperation of the first-, second-, and third-tier sub-national offices. The directors general of the regions meet every two months under the auspices of the general secretary of the Ministry of the Interior and consider the functioning of the offices of the region and possible solutions to problems.

These functions of the director general of the region are purely administrative. Regional power rests with the regional secretary, who is the highest regional official. The regional secretary supervises all offices of the *perifereia* and directs, coordinates, supervises, and examines the activity of the offices and the officials of the *perifereia*. He or she also has exclusive responsibility entrusted or transferred to the offices of the *perifereia* along with every other responsibility the law has provided or has entrusted. Among his or her responsibilities and powers is the supervision of local self-administration, which includes the municipalities, communities, prefectoral self-administration, and their legal personnel (Ministry of the Interior, Public Administration and Decentralization 1999). The regional secretary can transfer some responsibilities to the general directorate of the region, the supervising directorates, or the supervisors of officials of the regions. The regional secretary is assisted by the Office of the General Secretary of the Region, which organizes communication with the offices and the public and studies matters that come under the regional secretaries' jurisdiction.

Finally, the *perifereia* was assigned new responsibilities in the planning, programming, and implementation of economic, social, and cultural policies of development. Council membership changes slightly:

- the general secretary of the region as chair
- the presidents of the prefectoral self-administrations and the prefects of the region
- one representative from every local union of municipalities and communities of the region
- one representative of the regional organization of each of the Chambers of Productive Sectors, the Technical Chamber of Greece, the Geotechnical Chambers of Greece, the Economic Chamber of Greece, etc.
- the director general of the region, who does not vote (Article 1).

The regional council is responsible for designing, programming, and coordinating development of the *perifereia* within the framework of the democratic program (Ministry of the Interior, Local Governance, and Decentralization 1997). It is also the means of expression for local governments and the productive sectors (ibid.). In addition, the *perifereia* is given resources of its own; Article 4 places the general secretary of the region as the chief director of the budget for his or her region. The legislation states that as of 1998, the Ministry of the National Economy issues *Sillogikes Apofaseis Ergon Perifereieas* (SAEP), which are works of a regional character contained in the budget of the Public Investments.

They include work proposed exclusively by the regional council, work proposed by the regional council in collaboration with the responsible central authority, and work proposed by the responsible central authority and in accordance with the opinion the regional council. Provision is also made to allow the regional council, following the suggestion of the regional secretary, to transfer funds from one project to another, provided that they fall under the same category.

With the passage of Law 2647/1998, power was transferred to all three sub-national tiers. The law marked a significant step towards a more comprehensive administrative decentralization. Article 1 of Law 2647 outlines the powers that the ministries were to defer to the regions and prefectures, and provides for additional transfer of personnel from the first and second tiers of local government to the *perifereia* as well as from the *perifereia* to lower tiers. Under the new law, a transfer of power from the following ministries to the prefectoral level took place: the Ministry of Development, the Ministry of Education and Religion, the Ministry of Agriculture, the Ministry of Health and Welfare, the Ministry of Transport and Communication, and the Ministry of Public Order. However, as was the case with Law 2503, devolution is once again focused on the *perifereia* and occurred across all (or most) ministers. Certain responsibilities are divided or shared among the *perifereies*, prefectures, and the central administration. For instance, the maintenance of hospitals is the responsibility of the regional administration, while the supervision and monitoring of existing health clinics of the private sector is allocated to the prefectures and the centre.

Administrative and Political Schema

In effect, legislation established two regional tiers: one administrative and the other political. The thirteen *perifereies* of the third tier are, in essence, de-concentrated administrations and thus a new type of regional prefecture. On paper, they were given administrative responsibility, particularly in regional development. The result, as stated by the minister of the interior, was thirteen *mikres kiverniseis* (small governments) (*Ethnos*, 10 February 1997). The elected prefecture of the second tier became a new sub-national government.[9] Prefects in particular gained extensive powers, with elected status and considerable resources at their disposal. They now had offices, civil servants, and responsibility in licensing and commissioning local development projects. Initial analysis of the legislation indicates that before 1994 there were small but significant changes focused on the *perifereia*. In 1994, the legislation equally addressed the prefectures and the *perifereies*. After the 1997 period, however, the focus shifted exclusively to the *perifereia*. As the regional tier increased in importance, the prefecture decreased. This shift in emphasis corresponded to a shift in sub-national responsibility that was happening at the time in structural funds. Specifically, prefectoral and regional actors gained access to structural policy via the *regional* Council and *regional* monitoring committees. The regional council is described as the 'place of expression' of local governments and the representatives of the productive classes (Ministry of the Interior, Local Governance, and Decentralization 1997). In the chapters that follow, I argue that this shift created tension between the second- and third-tier actors. It also made for a complicated interconnectedness between levels as actors realized that to not cooperate would mean losing the opportunity to participate and to influence policy.

3 Europeanization as Political Adaptation to the Structural Programs (1989–1999)

Structural policy can be studied in three phases: the budgetary envelope, programming, and policy implementation. Although the first stage of policymaking can offer interesting research, the focus here is on policymaking as it pertains to programming and policy implementation. It is in these two stages that sub-national actors can enter the game and play the greatest role (interviews with Commission officials; Marks 1996).

Because of its complexity, the programming of structural funds demands a set procedure. For the 1989–93 period, programming was fixed for a five-year term and involved three stages: compilation of the Regional Development Plan (RDP); establishment of the Community Support Framework (CSF); and finally, the creation of Operational Programs.[1] Regional Development Plans were produced by each EU member state and were submitted to the European Commission. There was then bilateral negotiation between member states and the Commission that transformed these RDPs into a Community Support Framework once a version of the development plan was agreed upon. The CSFs coincided with the political regions for those member states where they existed, and administrative planning districts for those member states who introduced them following pressure from the Commission. Once the Operational Programs were approved by the Commission, the CSF became operational. This marked the end of preparation stage of planning. For the 1994–9 period, structural programming was made more flexible in that member states had the option of following a two-stage rather than the three-stage programming outlined above. Under the new approach, each EU member state drew up an RDP, which included specific economic programs. This was followed by negotiation of the CSF with the Commission and the establishment of a Single Programming Document (SPD). The result constrained the Commission because member states brought detailed plans rather than general statements, leaving less room to manoeuvre. It could also limit sub-national input because programs were submitted before general priorities were negotiated with the Commission. Marks (1996) argues that regional actors were aware of this and attempted to influence policy earlier in the process. This study led to similar conclusions; evidence suggests that regional actors are innovative and find routes of influence.

Implementation of the structural funds has been described as causing 'turbulence' to the Greek administrative system, an 'external shock,' and a 'threat to the pre-existing institutional arrangements' (Paraskevopoulos 2001). This chapter and the next examine how the Greek administrative model operated in practice by submitting it to two tests. Chapter 4 provides the normative test and outlines in more depth the findings of interviews of central, sub-national, and Commission officials. From these interviews, it was expected that the finer functioning of the political system would be understood and that some conclusions on how *ta politica* (the politics) were being played would be reached. This chapter provides the empirical test by examining policymaking, implementation, and performance in the Integrated Mediterranean Programs and in the first (1989–93) and second (1994–9) structural development programming periods.

If the administrative structures are in place, and if the political system is decentralized, performance of the structural funds should improve. If the working hypotheses proves correct, a quantitative and qualitative improvement in performance will be evident, and a qualitative improvement in centre–peripheral relations will emerge. The question to be addressed is what are the most useful factors in determining what makes a good policy. One aspect of performance is absorption rates. Although high absorption rates do not necessarily indicate good performance, and low rates of financial efficiency can be attributed to any number of factors, high rates should generally be seen as evidence of a well-functioning administration (interviews with Commission officials). There is also a qualitative aspect to performance that considers if program goals have been met, and if studies and comprehensive programs have taken precedence over the satisfaction of clientelist ends. Quality is determined by the findings in monitoring committee reports and in Commission documents, and from the responses of officials interviewed. Actors were identified from membership lists of monitoring committees. EU member states are obligated to describe management structures and procedures that monitor implementation of structural funds. That is, they have had to demonstrate *administrative capacity* of monitoring committees. Interviews with key players helped to determine who participated, and whether it was easy for the Commission to get Greek officials to adopt the Commission's priorities. If the central administration in Greece was indeed losing its hegemonic role in EU structural programs, an increased participation of sub-national actors would be apparent as the study moved from the IMPs to the CSFs.

The IMPs: A Cautious Step towards Decentralization

As noted earlier, the Integrated Mediterranean Programs were founded on the principles of subsidiarity and partnership among the Community, national, and regional authorities (Papageorgiou and Verney 1992). The IMPs stipulated that the programs be formulated and implemented 'at the relevant geographical levels' (Council Regulation, EEC 2088/5). Indeed, it can even be argued that the programs assumed the operation of sub-national planning authorities (Featherstone and Yannopoulos 1995). The problem was that in Greece there were no relevant geographical levels (Verney 1994). As a substitute, the Greek government had to invent a regional tier, and in 1985 the country was divided into six regions: the Aegean Islands, Crete, North Greece, West Greece and the Peloponnese, Central and East Greece, and Attica.

Another IMP stipulation was the existence of a development strategy for the region and a clear hierarchy of priorities that the program would strive to achieve (Plaskovitis 1994). The Greek administration, however, was not accustomed to such a comprehensive policy approach and consequently, the Greek IMPs were without such a development strategy (Plaskovitis 1994). The Ministry of the National Economy (MNE)[2] further compounded the problem by virtually ignoring the principles of subsidiarity and partnership. Although the MNE asked for input from government departments, central agencies, and prefects, the prefectoral and local actors were consulted unsystematically. The fact that many of the projects that the local actors recommended were small in scale (local road construction and school buildings) permitted the MNE officials to ignore many of the proposals, as they did not represent the type of regional development for which the programs were intended (Papageorgiou and Verney 1992). As a result, regional actors played only a minor role in drawing up the IMPs, and policymaking remained centralized.

Local politicians and interest group representatives complained about the hegemonic attitude of the MNE, but their complaints were not addressed. One could argue that the MNE was correct in its criticism and dismissal of the proposals. Indeed, many of the projects were more suitable for the clientelist ends of some of the local authorities. However, the complete lack of respect for the opinion of sub-national actors was hardly justified. Central agencies accepted this criticism but noted that the regions lacked adequate administrative and financial monitoring resources to provide either efficient planning or implementation (Papageorgiou and Verney 1992). What they failed to acknowledge, however, was that the administrative problems of the regions could have been corrected by central initiatives. In the end, so many of the prefects' proposals were rejected that the balance of projects went to central as opposed to regional work.

Implementation

The role played by sub-national actors did not improve in implementation. Responsibility for implementation of local measures was in theory intended to rest with the prefectures. But in practice, if a central agency was financing a measure, it was also responsible for implementation and it did not inform the prefecture on the progress of a measure. So the prefectures had no control over IMPs allocated to central agencies. Since the *perifereies* were not proper administrative bodies, they were no better positioned than the prefectures. Indeed, monitoring committees were the only regional structures established. The regions had no legislative identity, no resources, and no existence outside the IMPs. Their sole purpose was to facilitate the IMPs with monitoring committees (Featherstone and Yannopoulos 1995).

Apart from the secretariat, which comprised sub-program managers, Committee members included officials from public sector organizations, representatives of local interest groups, at least two European Commission officials, and in some cases prefects of the regions. Before the 1988 period, the committee was chaired by one of the prefects. Following the partial implementation of Law 1622, the regional secretary assumed the position of chair.[3] Committees were supposed to be linked to monitoring committees at the prefectoral levels, but these were usually not operational. When they did exist, there was a lack of cooperation and communication. Furthermore, there were no plans to link the prefectures into the IMP computer system that linked the regional offices of the MNE with the central administration which distributed information on implementation of the programs (Papageorgiou and Verney 1992).

Problems also arose because central agencies responsible for implementing the IMP measures and sub-programs were not in a position to set up studies or to appoint qualified staff to carry out the programs (Papageorgiou and Verney 1992). Surprisingly, the government's austerity program did not even foresee the need for additional staff. The only personnel allocated to the regions were the civil servants either on secondment from central ministries or serving part-time. It should be noted, however, that those civil servants selected were among the best in their areas of specialization. They were highly qualified, open-minded, and innovative – unusual characteristics of the civil service of that period (ibid.).

Difficulties were also encountered because regional monitoring committees had neither planning responsibility nor control over program implementation; they simply gathered information. The fact that they had no powers of revision was a serious shortcoming because the ability to make revisions as circumstances changed was an essential part of planning (Papageorgiou and Verney 1992). Since Greek administrators had neither previous planning experience nor clear priorities, issues that undoubtedly arose during implementation were unforeseen in the planning stage.[4] Even the region's limited role was plagued with problems. Although, on paper, the committees had the power to intervene and question implementing agencies, problems arose because they had no formal status in Greek law, no decision-making authority, and no authority to apply sanctions against officials who did not provide information or did not meet targets (ibid.). Their informal status meant that civil servants could not demand information and often had to 'beg for it' (ibid.).

In the end, monitoring committees met four times each year and reviewed the progress of the IMPs on the basis of information provided them by the secretariat. Again, there were difficulties. Sub-program managers were required to physically monitor the progress of programs, but they were not given the funding to do so. Consequently, they were forced to rely on second-hand information provided to them by the central agencies and the prefectoral-level civil servants. They often described their role as 'telephone operators' (Papageorgiou and Verney 1992). The main function of the committees became that of accountants, who concentrated on technical details, missing strategic points and attempting to maximize the financial absorption rate while overlooking developmental aspects (ibid.). This information, together with proposals for revision, was then passed to the Central Inter-Ministerial Committee in Athens, which could only revise up to 10 per cent of the IMP budget. More comprehensive revisions had to be taken to Brussels. This time-consuming process took at least a year to complete (ibid.). Not surprisingly, some members of IMP committees saw a need for direct communication with Brussels (ibid.).

Performance

The initial delay in the approval of the IMPs was compounded by a disappointing rate of implementation in the years that followed, and it created a huge time lag in the absorption of available resources (Plaskovitis 1994). By 1990, the IMPs had realized less than 50 per cent of the total planned expenditure and absorbed only 30 per cent of the total funding allocated to Greece (ibid.). Overall, attempts to centralize control were not beneficial to IMP performance. This 'zigzag' process was dysfunctional and inefficient in both time and effort (Papageorgiou and Verney 1992). Plaskovitis found a number of administrative shortcomings: a lack of expertise and inappropriate staffing, co-responsibility between different bureaucratic authorities, and weak preparatory studies that translated into implementation delays. The consensus arising from these results was the need for an increased role for the *periphereies* in planning and coordinating the development programs. To accomplish this, regional administrations needed independence, authority, and resources (interviews with Commission officials). It is interesting that those IMP measures that were controlled and financed by local agencies were found to perform much better in absorption and final results (Papageorgiou and Verney).

Effects of the IMPs on Decentralization and Administration

Plaskovitis (1994) argues that the political decision to cover the regions and sectors without exception meant that there was 'minimal structural impact.'[5] On a similar note, a study ending in 1989 found that not one of the thirty-five 'central interviewees referred to the role of the regions in relation to Greece's European prospects and to the single market' (Papageorgiou and Verney 1992, 158). In addition, only two of the twenty national public agency officials saw decentralization as a possible effect of the IMPs (ibid.). So it appears that even in the late 1980s, a top-down approach was not considered an impediment to either the planning or the implementation of structural programs. Since central elites did not see a need for devolution, they were unprepared to give up their hegemonic position. On the other hand, considering the long history of centralization, the committees, though in many respects empty shells and lacking significant powers, were an administratively novel process (Ioakimidis 1996b; Papageorgiou and Verney; Plaskovitis 1994). Further, unlike the unfulfilled promise of elections at the prefectoral level, which was not linked to EU programs, the regional aspect of Law 1622 – which was linked – was slowly but tentatively taking shape in 1988. Considering the above, it can be argued that EC development programs began to 'breathe life into the regions' (Verney 1994). The argument can also be made that the experience of the IMPs 'raised in a more urgent form the question of a transfer of power from the Centre to the periphery' (Papageorgiou and Verney, 154).

Approaching the question from the bottom up, Papageorgiou and Verney (1992) write that there was a 'silent revolution' in centre–periphery relations. To begin with, monitoring committees helped forge links between sub-national actors and Commission officials, and the presence of Commission officials gave sub-national actors confidence (Ioakimidis 1996b; Papageorgiou and Verney). Another bit of evidence pointing towards improved centre–periphery relations was that regional respondents considered the implementation of the IMPs a useful learning experience. Monitoring and progress reports were 'radical concepts' and 'unusual practice' for the Greek civil service (Papageorgiou and Verney). It is surprising, given their qualifications, that the secretariat of the monitoring committees complained of a 'superiority complex' of the Athens-based civil servants towards them (ibid.). Despite this negativity, implementation of the IMPs appeared to give regional civil servants confidence.

The secretariat complained of the negative attitude of government and bureaucrats towards new ideas. They also criticized the parochial quality of the local politicians and interest groups who tried to secure funds for their constituencies or sector without concern for the program as a whole. Hence, the secretariat were critical of both upper- and lower-level officials, perhaps because of 'differences' in qualification and training. It may also be evidence of a slow emergence of a new elite within the administration. Papageorgiou and Verney (1992) argued that as long as the careers of the regional secretaries depended on their obedience to the centre, they could not be voices for the region. But while this may have been correct in the late 1980's, the same argument could not be made in the 1990s (interviews with central and regional officials). Findings here indicate that regional secretaries started to see themselves as representatives, not of central government, but of their respective regions.

First Community Support Framework, 1989–1993

Policymaking and the State of Decentralization

Problems encountered with the IMPs were partly acknowledged in regulations of the structural funds. In many respects, the IMPs demonstrated 'how not to plan' (Nanetti 1996; Plaskovitis 1994). Greek authorities had to also familiarize themselves with a host of new concepts and practices. Take the example of 'additionality,' which stipulated that regions would lose funds if the state did not appropriate and release matching amounts efficiently – a concept that put added emphasis on the need for administrative reform. Another example of new ideas with which authorities had to familiarize themselves was the 'integrated approach,' a practice wherein public and private actors collaborated on territorially defined, medium-term development programs that made sense in regional contexts. The integrated approach is noteworthy for expanding the reliance on formal studies and expert opinions. Finally, greater regard for the principle of 'subsidiarity' as advocated by the Commission required that regional actors get involved in implementation and to some extent in decision-making as well.

Negotiation of the Greek Regional Development Program (*Schedio Perifereiakis Anaptixis*) was time-consuming. While other EU member states had their Community Support Framework approved by October 1989, the Greek CSF was not concluded until March 1990. The CSF for Objective 1 (see table 3.1) covered the entire country and consisted of two types of programs: national programs, reflecting the argument that Greece as a whole was a less-favoured region; and regional programs comprising the thirteen Regional Operational Programs (*Perifereiaka Epichirisiaka Programmata*, or PEPs), one for each of the thirteen *perifereies*.[6] When the RDPs were being compiled, the *perifereies* as outlined in Law 1622 were in force, but they had not yet assumed a coherent administrative schema. Regional secretaries were appointed in 1988, but as noted earlier, there was no devolution of administrative functions to the regional level, nor was there a proper administration at the regional level. The decentralized services of government ministries had been re-organized to correspond to the new regions, but these regions had not been allocated personnel of their own. Regional committees were formed ad hoc, bringing together central, prefectoral, and Commission officials to monitor implementation of the programs.

So there was no devolution of administrative functions at the regional level analogous to what took place in the prefectures in the 1980s. The regional level of administration, if it can be labelled as such at that time, had fewer responsibilities than the prefectures, which were still de-concentrated units of the centre. Further, new personnel were needed but were not placed in the prefectoral administrations. Considering these facts, it is surprising to note that the European Commission's *Second Annual Report* (1990) states that the regional sections of the thirteen multi-fund operational programs allowed Greek actors at the regional level a major role. In reality, national ministries dominated the CSF process, and the regionalization promoted by the Commission still faced considerable opposition by the centre. In policymaking, it is immediately apparent that cooperation or a tri-partite partnership among the Commission, national, and sub-national officials was far from established.

Once again, the Ministry of the National Economy controlled policy-making; it had sole authority to decide on the context of regional pro-grams and could ignore regional input. The argument can be made that since they were political appointees, regional secretaries could be by-passed with impunity. But a more plausible explanation is that the re-gions were new incarnations and were not functioning administrations, so regional actors could not exert their demands. This latter point is elaborated upon below and in the next chapter. Regional authorities were instructed to submit proposals to be included in the Regional Development Plans; these proposals were then assessed by regional councils and submitted to the MNE for final approval. The MNE found only a small percentage of the RDPs acceptable but did include them in the final program. Ultimately, 60 per cent of the funds were allocated to large-scale (national) programs of a horizontal nature (transportation, telecommunications, energy infrastructure projects, etc.), and 40 per cent were allocated to the thirteen Regional Development Programs that cor-responded to the regions established under Law 1622. There are three explanations for this division. First, there was a priority attached to con-vergence: the primary concern of the central administration was to at-tain the per-capita income of other EU countries, so equitable regional

Table 3.1
Financial implementation in Greece of Objective 1 CSF 1989–1993*

	ECUs (millions) (1993 prices) 1989–93	%
Updated assistance planned (A)	7,496,50	
Payments 1993 (B)	1,891,34	
Commitments 1993 (C)	1,795,22	
Payments (B2)	6,383,00	
Commitments (C2)	7,570,54	
B/C		105.0
B2/C2		84,0
C2/A		101.0

CSF 1994–1999**

	ECUs (millions) 1994–9	%
Assistance (A)	14,341,90	
Payments 1999 (B)	1,896,43	
Commitments 1999 (C)	2,749,63	
Payments 1994–9 (B2)	10,608,95	
Commitments 1994–9 (C2)	14,380,15	
B/C		69
B2/C2		74
C2/A		100

* Source: European Commission, 1993.
** European Commission, 1999.

development assumed a lesser importance. Second, it was politically important that funds be absorbed quickly and, despite the fact that regional projects had a better performance rate with the IMPs, the central administration still believed that it would be easier to show a high absorption rate on large-scale projects of a national dimension (Ioakimidis 1996; Plaskovitis 1994).[7] So the MNE chose the fastest and safest projects. It can be argued, however, that the overall emphasis on infrastructure such as transport and telecommunications, rather than on projects aimed at improving the quality of life, was sound reasoning, since the recipient regions were lagging behind in this respect. Third, and perhaps most justifiable, central actors feared that regional notables would use this funding to further clientelist purposes and scatter the funds for small-scale projects. To safeguard against this possibility, the Ministry of the National Economy attempted to centralize the programs (Ioakimidis).

Implementation

The actual text of the Community Support Framework stipulated that monitoring committees would operate at the regional level; this was in response to the European Commission, which expressed reservations about the ability of the regional tier to implement Operational Programs. In response, the Greek government established thirteen monitoring committees.[8] Authorities responsible for formal implementation as outlined in the Regional Operational Programs (described in detail below) included the offices of the ministries, sub-national authorities (primarily prefectures), and development associations.

Verney (1994, 172) argues that at this stage, structural policy 'began to force a change in government practice.' The operative word here is *began*. Although attempts to satisfy partnership requirements at the point of implementation were better in comparison to the IMP experience, they did not proceed very far. Decisions on projects of national magnitude were centralized at the ministerial level, while the prefectures decided on regional matters. The 60:40 differentiation between national and regional projects allowed the central administration to maintain the balance of control over how policies and programs were put into practice. Implementation below the centre was concentrated primarily at the prefectoral level, but the prefectures were still deconcentrated units of the centre. An additional challenge for the prefectures was the fact that they were not as well organized as the *perifereies* later become and were geographically too small to undertake the level of coordination and planning that was needed for the Community OPs (interviews with Commission and regional officials). The *perifereies* themselves were not institutionally strong, nor were they well developed, and they could not play a significant role in implementation.

The primary function of the *perifereies* was still the monitoring of programs implemented from the outside. Monitoring committees were chaired by the general secretary of the region and included as members the prefects of the region, representatives of the local self-administration, representatives of the Ministry of the National Economy, the Ministry of Agriculture, the Ministry of Labour, etc., representatives from DG XVI of the EU Commission, and members of the secretariat. Monitoring committees secured the correct implementation of the projects and ensured that programs were properly instituted. They allowed the *perifereies* to perform this task more systematically than the IMPs. In particular, monitoring committees introduced new management mechanisms such as the private managers expert firms to assist with aspects of the Operational Programs. The MNE, however, retained its central position. It administered *payments* and maintained financial control. In theory, the monitoring committees modified and adapted the programs. They could propose changes to the Operational Programs, but they were still beholden to the state and the EU Commission (interviews with senior civil servants). Despite their increased involvement in internal processes, in practice, regional staff and monitoring committees were still marginalized, and their ability to influence implementation was significantly compromised.

Overall Performance

Member states and the EU Commission produce annual reports on implementation of structural programs. These evaluations take into account quantitative data having to do with the absorption of funds and qualitative data pertaining to the performance of programs. The normative aspect of Commission reports includes the Commission's opinion on adherence to the partnership principle. This is particularly useful because it provides an external, perhaps objective observation. Quantitative data are linked to the budget implementation at the EU level, which provides an overview of *commitments* and *payments*. *Commitments* are figures indicating that projects have been identified and have been approved. *Payments* are said to have taken place once a cheque is signed by the Commission. Financial efficiency, as it is represented by *payments/commitments*, is a particularly informative source (interviews with Commission officials). Credit for particular projects is granted only when the project has been designed, approved, and implemented, and after the Commission's auditors are convinced that correct accounting procedures have been followed.

Year-by-year data are obviously useful in assessing the performance of structural programs, but it must be remembered that most programs are part of a multi-year schema and thus annual assessments are not completely reliable. For this reason, evaluation reports provide annual data as well as cumulative figures. The Commission's budgetary commitments are fixed in annual instalments: a first instalment is fixed following the decision to adopt the program, and subsequent instalments are based on the financing plan and the completion of actions. So while it can be argued that in the final year of a programming period *commitments* should be relatively high in terms of percentage, one cannot argue that in the mid-term, *commitments* or *payments* should be at 50 per cent (interviews with Commission officials). Indeed, in the beginning, there is a need for projections, time is needed to set up committees, and some projects require longer implementation periods than others. However, as projects move closer to the final years of the CSF, the figures should be fairly indicative of success or failure. That is, *commitments* in the final year should be relatively high in perhaps the eightieth to ninetieth percentile (ibid.).

Member state evaluations of performance are also very useful, for they provide researchers with an internal, perhaps subjective interpretation of how member state administrators perceive their successes, failures, and problems. They also offer an internal look at the functioning of these administrations, given that these reports often cite the problems and frustrations encountered by sub-national actors. This is particularly important, because there is no single standardized evaluation methodology to which member state administrations must adhere. Rather, a wide range of methods should be customized so that they match the particular needs and situation of each program. The methodologies applied by evaluators vary in nature and quality from one program to another. In effect, 'evaluations were expected to provide the data necessary to assist monitoring committees to form an opinion and propose corrective measures to the relevant authorities so as to enable adjustments to be made to the programs' (European Commission 1999). The challenge is to 'reinforce evaluation as a genuine tool for decision-making, strengthening monitoring and indicator systems, supporting evaluation methodologies and promoting a multilateral exchange of experience across the European Union' (ibid.).[9]

Considering the delay in approval of funds, the degree of central control, and the shortcomings of the regional administration, problems in implementation would be expected, but numerical data and Commission reports were favourable. Indeed, 1991 was declared a 'particularly important year for implementing the Greek CSF in that there was a significant acceleration in the rate of implementation of the operational measures as well as the adoption of almost all the planned Operational Programs' (European Commission, *Third Annual Report* 1991). Further, substantial progress was made in upgrading basic regional infrastructure (roads, water supply networks, drainage); in mobilizing local initiatives and in stimulating research and technology capacity; in establishing support services for SMEs; and in realizing large-scale infrastructure projects (European Commission 1993). Thessaloniki was noted for mobilizing local initiatives and stimulating research and technology capacity; Patra had a reputation for establishing support services for SMEs; and the Athens Metro and motorways such as Athens-Corinth and Athens-Thessaloniki were noted as successful large-scale infrastructure projects (interviews with Commission officials).

At the end of 1993, 93 per cent of the total funds of the Greek CSF had been spent, leaving only a small balance of expenditure to be paid in 1994. Commission officials considered this figure very satisfactory. Greece had fully committed its planned assistance. In payments/ commitments, Greece was at 84 per cent, and payments continued in the post-1993 period so that overall figures for payments increased. Hence, 1993 figures of less than the hundredth percentile in payments/ commitments do not indicate a negative performance. What is important is that commitments were made and projects were identified. The CSF for 1989–93 was effectively closed in 1994 with an implementation rate of almost 100 per cent.

In Regional Operational Programs, the annual rate of implementation increased from 60 per cent to more than 95 per cent between 1990 and 1991. Part of the explanation for improvement in implementation of the CSF compared to the IMPs was the joint effort of the Commission and member state to implement the program. As the programming period progressed, administrative operations were rationalized and modern management mechanisms for project monitoring were introduced. The experience acquired in programming and management indicated a need to establish within agencies, ministries, and other public bodies, cells of officials familiar with procedures that would provide a more solid base for preparation of the second phase of programming. Further, program managers were being employed to help regional administrations manage regional programs. The increased local presence of the Commission in the form of on-site assistance from Commission experts made available to regional authorities was helpful in drafting measures to promote the development of SMEs in regional programs.[10] By 1993, training and employment programs conformed to what was programmed and the 'modernization of the public administration' reached 'cruising speeds' (European Commission, *Fourth Annual Report* 1993).

Experience was also being gained in monitoring and assessing regional and sectoral programs and in the application of multi-annual financial programming. In addition, as the programming period progressed, the regions were acquiring greater weight as they were called upon to become quasi-partners of central government and of the Commission. It is interesting to note that in the end, regional projects had a better absorption rate than national projects (Ioakimidis 1996; Plaskovitis 1994). It is apparent from these signs of progress that time was needed for the Greek administration to become acquainted with and accustomed to the new approach that structural policy demanded.

The Experience of the Regions: A Mixed Verdict

The focus here is on the Regional Operational Programs, which are part of the regional section of the CSF for Greece and include three funds: the European Regional Development Fund (ERDF), the European Social Fund (ESF), and the European Agricultural Guidance and Guarantee Fund (EAGG-F). These programs seek to improve basic infrastructures, reinforce the primary sectors, improve the competitiveness of enterprise, and protect the environment (see Appendix A). Total community support for Central Macedonia was set at 294,3 million European Currency Units (ECUs); for West Greece this figure was set at 98,0 million ECUs (see table 3.2).

By the end of 1993, planned assistance was fully committed for the Regional Operational Programs of both West Greece and Central Macedonia (see table 3.2). Total payments to commitments indicated that West Greece was at 99 per cent while Central Macedonia was slightly lower at 91 per cent (see table 3.2). However, the problem was that for the CSF (1989–93), the rate of absorption took priority as a measure of success (interviews with Commission officials and with upper-level civil servants in the MNE). As a result, there were problems encountered on other levels. The final report (Ministry of the National Economy 1996) for Central Macedonia concluded that since the *perifereia* was at the initial stages of organization and operation, it encountered significant problems in the implementation of the programs. Difficulties were attributed partly to a 'lack of indicative political organization at the regional level' and 'inadequate cooperation between national and regional authorities for the planning preparation efforts which are materialized in the *perifereia* and enlisted in various other functioning programs and Community Initiatives' (ibid.).

Problems also occurred with Subprogram EAPTA[11] – a division of the sub-program of the PEP for Central Macedonia for work of the local level. However, the Ministry of the Interior considered the sub-program as a program of the ministry, and enlisted, modified, and replaced the work of the sub-program almost always without the corresponding

Table 3.2
CSF 1: 1989–1993 financial implementation of regional operational programs

| | ECUs (millions) 1993 | | % | |
	OP Central Macedonia	OP West Greece	OP Central Macedonia	OP West Greece
Assistance (A)	294,3	98,0		
Payments (B)	94,5	31,7		
Commitments (C)	105,1	31,3		
Payments 1989–93 (B2)	268,7	97,2		
Commitments 1989–93 (C2)	294,3	98,0		
B/C			89.93	101.25
C2/A			100.00	99.99
B2/A			91.29	99.27
B2/C2			91.29	99.27

Sources: Ministry of the National Economy, 1990, 1996.

decision of the general secretary of the region. In other words, the Ministry of the Interior bypassed the regional secretary, and the result was a marked difference between the original approved budget for the measure and its final form. There were also problems in securing funding for projects. The entanglement in the proceedings of many actors (prefecture, Ministry of the Interior, Treasury Reserve and Loans) contributed to the delay of *payments* so that contract work risked being cancelled or interrupted. Finally, in the sub-program *efarmogi* (implementation), there were delays because the secretariat of the monitoring committee was not properly informed about the *payments* and modifications of the MNE (interviews with officials in Central Macedonia). Findings of monitoring committees stressed the importance of a clear institutional structure granting decentralized powers to the *perifereiu* so that it could undertake the economic management and make decisions needed to implement projects (Ministry of the National Economy 1996). Additionally, the positions of all actors needed to be clarified, so the objective of each position, the qualifications of personnel, and the obligation of the implementing authorities opposite the monitoring committee and the secretariat were defined.

The overall progress of the programs for Western Greece was deemed relatively satisfactory (Ministry of the National Economy 1990). However, there were problems similar to those experienced by Central Macedonia. Again, there were difficulties attributed to a lack of studies, improper training of personnel, and inexperience with the type of programs being implemented. Indeed, particularly in the early years of this programming period, studies were considered unnecessary by the sub-national administration. Further, the argument in the next chapter is that the lack of comprehensive studies permitted officials to 'attach' works to larger projects, thereby satisfying clientelist ends.

Second Community Support Framework: 1994–1999

In order to draft the second Regional Development Plan, a more formal inter-ministerial coordinating committee was established within the MNE. But the committee comprised officials only from the central government, with no regional representation within this elite circle of policymakers. A small group of high-ranking civil servants formed the secretariat, and they prepared the preliminary draft. The committee was chaired by the secretary general of the MNE responsible for regional development. Regional secretaries were asked to draft proposals, set up working groups, and seek input from other public agencies and the private sector. Where regional secretaries established working groups of technocrats and experts, participation from the prefectures and local government remained limited (interview with MNE official; Ioakimidis 1996). Further, although the committee appeared willing to invite some regional input, the MNE found a way to dominate the process (Ioakimidis). To begin, regional authorities had to work out their proposals within a very tight framework defined beforehand by the MNE. The government had declared that a large portion of the funds would go to a few large projects (the Athens Metro, the Athens Airport, and major highways). This meant that instead of 40 per cent of the funds going to the regions, only 30 per cent was designated for regional development. This allocation of funds reflected party pressure and political considerations. So, from a central perspective, clientelism was still playing a significant role. Further, the centre determined what percentage would go to which region. The claim was that the allocation was based on socio-economic criteria established by the Centre for Planning and Research (KEPE). KEPE scrutinized the proposals and drew up a comprehensive draft; the plan was then put together by a small team of experts under the chairmanship of the deputy minister of the MNE.

The entire process took place between November 1992 and August 1993. Ioakimidis (1996) argues that there was no genuine synergy among central, regional, and local authorities, for the primary concern of the centre was to formulate a proposal that would be accepted by the

Commission, and the notion of participatory planning was down-played. This can be attributed to feelings of superiority of the central civil service, and the MNE's anxiety to preserve its hegemony. It was also a result of the weak institutional position of sub-national actors. The fact that the principal regional interlocutors were centrally ap-pointed secretaries meant that they could not resist the hegemonic ten-dencies of the central bureaucrats (ibid.). So regional secretaries had to bow to the central authorities who had the economic resources and the political authority to make and impose decisions (ibid.). Indeed, viewed from this perspective, one can argue that the RDPs had a centralizing effect, since they provided the centre with new instruments to control local and regional authorities. However, the control of the MNE was slowly being questioned. When 60 per cent of the proposals submitted by regional authorities were rejected, modified, or replaced, there was a marked reaction from the periphery (ibid.). The lack of respect for the regional proposals brought harsh criticism from opposition parties and regional authorities. The RDP had been submitted to the EU Commission in September 1993 as the basis for negotiation of the new CSF, but when PASOK came to power in October 1993, it asked the Commission for permission to revise the RDP (ibid.). Consequently, this delayed the CSF process.

The CSF adopted by the Commission on 13 July 1994 (see table 3.1) included thirteen regional OPs and fifteen multi-regional OPs. There was a marked attempt to incorporate the experience from the previous programming period into the new programs. To begin with, Greek of-ficials realized that absorption of a large volume of funding did not guarantee results of high quality (interviews with Commission offi-cials). Further, greater importance was attached to improving the mechanisms for implementation, including substitution of the private sector for the public sector and greater decentralization of responsibili-ties for programming and implementation so that the region's locally generated potential could be developed. Finally, compared to the for-mer CSF, there was a more ambitious approach, with such policies as environment and quality of life gaining greater emphasis (interviews with Commission officials).

Implementation

As the programs were being implemented, the administrative reforms outlined in the previous chapter were being introduced. On a purely administrative level, new management techniques were introduced to improve managerial capabilities of the regions and ministries. For example, the Management Organization Unit (MOU) was established to provide expert personnel and know-how to implement national CSF operational programs. MOU was a support mechanism, operating under the guidance and control of MNE, but it was external to the civil service structure. It assisted public administration by covering specific needs in human resources and know-how to implement CSF operational programs that exceeded the technical and administrative capacity of the implementing authorities (organization of management, training of personnel, transfer of know-how, and provision of organizational tools). In addition, the use of project data sheets as programming tools was extended to all CSF programs. Further, at the insistence of the EU Commission, there was greater incorporation of the private sector to help analyse and conduct studies (Spanou 1998). On the one hand, the hiring of private consultants for Regional Operating Programs was a substitute for administrative inefficiencies (Christofilopoulou 1996). The same argument can be made for the special agency for the management of the Community Support Framework (Law 2375/1996). On the other hand, these changes were believed to improve overall performance and to ensure the correct materialization of the programs to implement outlined goals (interviews with the MNE). This also encouraged the public sector to adopt new methods of operation by allowing them to witness the advantages of new techniques (ibid.).

The newly decentralized structure required the cooperation of many authorities, which varied, depending on the sub-program and measure in question. Those responsible for implementation were offices of the central ministries, the decentralized offices of the regional administration, the prefectures, the local level, and private enterprises, legal persons, and enterprises of the wider public sector. In the period prior to 1998, implementation was primarily the responsibility of central and prefectoral administrations, while the role of the region was to coordinate and monitor the programs. The regional secretary's responsibility was *na eleghe* (to monitor), scrutinizing and examining the functioning of lower tiers. However, as argued in the next chapter, this is not to suggest that the regional secretary had limited influence. The regional secretary had access to central administrators and his or her presence was understood by prefectoral authorities. So, even though the *perifereia* may not have been directly implementing the programs, there may have been improvement in performance that can be attributed to the region. In 1998 emphasis shifted, so the *perifereia* became the centre of focus. The *Perifereiako Tameio Anaptixis* (Regional Treasury of Development) as outlined in Law 2218 became operational. This made the *perifereia* the cashier of works. Further, a pilot project giving planning powers was introduced in four *perifereies*: Central Macedonia, Peloponnisos, Crete, and Thessaly. It entailed 250 ERDF projects on fifteen to twenty studies intended to improve regional development. Regional authorities submitted their proposals, funding was approved by the appropriate ministry, and the project was implemented by the *perifereia*. The approval of proposals was only a formality (interviews with MNE officials). The MNE was responsible for inter-ministerial coordination; its representatives on the monitoring committees monitored the progress of implementation and gave out funding as the projects evolved. When this form of decentralization was found to be functioning well, the central ministry decided in 1999 to expand the policy to include the remaining *perifereies* (interviews with MNE officials).

Although some ministry officials were reluctantly cooperating with the new decentralized approach, as implementation progressed, central *and* regional authorities were administering the programs. Indeed, 40 to 50 per cent of planification in the post-pilot period was the responsibility of the region (interview with Commission official). Further, the *perifereies* were in a better position to monitor, for they had an expanded personnel and functioning administrative structures. In addition, the fact that regional secretaries were well qualified and trained meant that they were able to handle the challenge and the opportunity that their new powers presented. The secretariats of the monitoring committees wrote up the monetary register and progress reports every six months, and they helped activate slow or delayed actors in implementing projects. The committee had the power to modify the Operational Programs in accordance with representatives of the competent office of the state and the Commission of the EU, as outlined in the CSF. The monitoring committee decided on financing measures, but increases to the approved figures required approval of the regional secretary (chair of the monitoring committee), so the regional secretary's role was of considerable importance. The argument made in the next chapter is that, despite the fact the regional secretaries are political appointees, they have been able to mould a role for themselves; they are voices for their region, and within the realm of EU programs they attempt to provide a check on the practice of clientelism.

Overall Performance of the Greek CSF (1994–1999)

The Commission found that 'since 1994, Greece has made big progress putting the European Union's Structural Funds into action ... the mid-term review concludes that the Greek performance, after a slow start, is improving in leaps and bounds in most areas' (European Commission 1998). Further, 1996 was considered to be a turning point in implementation of the CSF in Greece. By the end of the year, financial implementation of the Greek CSF reached the average of the Objective 1 countries, and it was expected that this 'satisfactory rate of implementation should gather pace in 1997' (European Commission 1996). The 1998 report also noted that there 'was a fast rhythm of absorption coupled with good implementation quality ... the Greek absorption rate ... is now higher than the average of all EU countries' (European Commission 1998b). And in 1999, 'the rate of utilization of the CSF appropriations continued to accelerate' (European Commission 2000). The overall progress was attributed to 'the efficient work of the implementing agencies for the larger CSF projects and to a series of decisions made by the monitoring committees' (ibid.).

It appears that the increased administrative powers that were afforded to the regions had a positive impact on implementation. The power of monitoring committees to make decisions and to make transfers within programs was also a key factor in performance. But there were still lingering problems. A review of the reports of the monitoring committees and findings from interviews indicates that these claims were somewhat over-optimistic, at least for the period before 1997–8. As is argued below, problems arose because regional offices, especially the smaller ones, were still without sufficient personnel and had limited operational possibilities. Further, at times, the organizational and functional weaknesses of the regional staff led to fruitless decisions, unrealistic proposals, and delays in *payments*. In addition, the central administration was unable to provide quick solutions, and this resulted in delays.

The Experience of the Regions: A Slow but Definite Improvement

Total Community support for the Regional Operational Program was set at 609,0 million ECUs for Central Macedonia (Appendix B and table 3.3), and at 295,1 million ECUs for West Greece (Appendix C and table 3.3). Differences in funding reflect differences in geographical size and

Table 3.3
CSF 2: 1994–1999 implementation of regional operational programs

	ECUs (millions) 1994–9		%	
	Central Macedonia	West Greece	Central Macedonia	West Greece
Assistance (A)	609,0	295,1		
Payments 1999 (B)	87,3	33,5		
Commitments 1999 (C)	159,6	64,0		
Payments 1994–9 (B2)	464,0	203,8		
Commitments 1994–9 (C2)	604,6	286,7		
B/C			55	52
C2/A			99	97
B2/A			76	69
B2/C2			77	71

Sources: European Commission, 1999a; offices of the *perifereies* of Central Macedonia and West Greece.

population. Regional actors in West Greece in general, and Achaia in particular, however, were not satisfied with the amount of funding they were receiving (interview with regional officials in West Greece; interview with prefect of Achaia).

In general, Central Macedonia had a relatively good completion rate for most of its programs. Similarly, it was noted that the rate of implementation of the OP for West Greece gained momentum, even though there was a variety and a complexity in the problems encountered (Ministry of the National Economy 1997). At the end of 1999, Central Macedonia had committed 99 per cent of its planned assistance, while West Greece was slightly lower at 97 per cent (see table 3.3). So Central Macedonia moved ahead of West Greece for the Second Programming Period. The same can be said for *payments*: Central Macedonia had paid out 77 per cent of its total *commitments* while West Greece had paid out 71 per cent (see table 3.3). As is seen below, this progress can be attributed to Central Macedonia's administration. As argued earlier, however, differences in *payments* do not necessarily translate into better or less favourable performance in the Greek regions. Indeed, with CSF (1989–93), absorption in Greece was quite high, but there were other problems. Empirical data must be considered within a broader perspective. So again, it was important to establish how the administration was performing on other levels.

In Western Greece, the second structural programs were better implemented than the first in both quality and absorption rates (interview with secretary of the Monitoring Committee for West Greece). The explanation for this improved performance is that under the first CSF, the *perifereies* were relatively new conceptions. With the second CSF, the *perifereies* had acquired a more established role (interview with officials from MNE).[12] There were, however, problems attributed to delays in the approval of works that were dependent on ministry authorities and were implemented by the decentralized offices/services. Policy implementation was believed to be too centralized, and the institutional structures were still deficient (interviews with officials in West Greece *Perifereia*). A case study undertaken in West Greece in 1998 found that authorities responsible for implementing the regional Operational Programs believed that the absence of the *Perifereiako Tameio* (Regional Treasury) had harmed programs implemented at the regional level. So the degree of decentralization, as it applied to administration and programming, was considered to be limited. The study discovered problems with the flow of funds and with the ministerial approval of certain works (Ministry of the National Economy 1996). In addition, there were delays because the works were not characterized as regional, national, or prefectoral (ibid.). There were also problems in the quality of projects that were attributed to a lack of extensive studies. Finally, individuals who implemented the sub-programs all agreed that with the exception of the regional Operational Programs, there was a lack of communication with central authorities. The information given was entirely symptomatic. Only in cases where there were problems with implementing measures of other projects would regional actors and the MNE turn to the general secretary as a political figure having responsibility (ibid.). By the spring of 2000, there were ongoing difficulties with quality in approximately half of the projects of West Greece's OP (interviews with Commission officials), but the situation was improving (interviews with Commission officials): the monitoring committee noted that the majority of the organizational, administrative, and *thesmika* (institutional) problems that affected the implementation of programs had been overcome (Ministry of the National Economy 2000). It was expected that these changes would have a positive impact on the programs in the years to come (ibid.).

Quality of performance was better in Central Macedonia than in West Greece, which is attributed to the decentralization reforms and to the special circumstances in Central Macedonia's administration (interviews with officials in MNE and Ministry of the Interior; Ministry of the National Economy 1999). That is, since the ministry of Macedonia and Thrace is located in Thessaloniki, it was relatively simple to transfer some personnel to the regional administration. As a result, Central Macedonia has some of the best qualified personnel of all the *perifereies* and hence was expected to perform better (interview with Ministry of the Interior upper-level civil servant). The administrative changes, the devolved responsibilities of the centre, and the hiring of qualified personnel such as engineers and other experts had a 'distinct impact' on the OPs of Central Macedonia (interviews with Commission officials). There was, however, a need for additional changes, more personnel, and further decentralization (interviews with Commission officials). For example, the monitoring institutions were working well, but further improvements were needed at the prefectoral level. There were also problems attributed to incomplete studies and to institutional and horizontal organizational/coordination. For example, there were delays in issuing enforceable decisions from the ministries on whose basis the *perifereia* would pronounce programs (Ministry of the National Economy 1999).[13] Problems were also encountered with measures entailing innovation, but this can be expected and should not be considered a major shortcoming of the Greek administration (interviews with Commission officials).

Overall, the implementation and monitoring of the projects of the PEPs of both West Greece and Central Macedonia was considered to be comprehensive (interviews Commission officials). In the course of the five-year implementation period, there was a clearer role for private actors as consultants and monitoring assistants. Further, the majority of those implementing the programs had *learned* from the many years of working with the programs. There was considerable cross-checking, examination, and study undertaken so that performance could be more accurately assessed. Evidence in the next chapter further suggests a change in the general attitude of the administration so that studies are increasingly seen as important. This can challenge clientelism and the practice of 'attachments' because it involves a more comprehensive approach to programming, so funds are not scattered to satisfy small-scale works with clientelist ends. So, unlike the first CSF, where the maximization of the rate of absorption was the only criterion for success, in the latter part of the 1990s, Greek authorities were acknowledging the connection between studies and qualitative performance, and qualitative factors were increasingly being used to measure success (interviews with Commission officials; officials from central and regional administrations). In addition, there was extensive dialogue and communication between members of the monitoring committee involving a tri-member (region–centre–EU) relationship, which was productive. Development was defined as 'reaching the goals of the programs through cooperation and partnership with sub-national actors' (interviews with MNE officials). The role of MNE officials in monitoring committees was simply to observe that the system was functioning properly. Hence, central authorities assumed an unobtrusive role and allowed the regional secretary and sub-national actors to take the lead.

Conclusions

Moving from the IMPs, to the first CSF (1989–93), and finally to the second CSF (1994–9), there has been an increased role permitted subnational actors, and a corresponding increased attempt at administrative decentralization, as is evident in the establishment of the *perifereies*, and their qualitative performance has improved. In the IMPs, there were administrative shortcomings: a lack of expertise and inappropriate staffing, co-responsibility between different bureaucratic authorities, and weak preparatory studies. Further, centralization created inefficiencies in time and effort, which translated into implementation delays. It is interesting that even in the late 1980s, a top-down approach was not considered an impediment to either the planning or the implementation of structural programs. For the first CSF (1989–93), national ministries still dominated planning, and the regionalization promoted by the Commission was still resisted by the centre. Even though attempts to satisfy partnership requirements at the point of implementation were better, in comparison to the IMP experience, they did not proceed very far. Implementation below the centre was primarily at the prefectoral level, but the prefectures were still de-concentrated units of the centre. Further, they were not as well organized as the *perifereies* later became and were geographically too small to undertake the coordination and planning that was needed for the Community OPs. Although the Greek regions' performance from a numerical perspective was very satisfactory, the rate of absorption took priority as a measure of success. As a result, there were problems encountered on other levels. For example, difficulties were attributed to a 'lack of organization at the regional level and to inadequate cooperation between national and regional authorities for the planning preparation efforts' (interviews with Commission officials). In the case of the second CSF (1994–9), the centre appeared more willing to invite some regional input, but the MNE still dominated the process. The primary concern of the centre was the formulation of a proposal that would be acceptable to the Commission, so the notion of participatory planning was downplayed. Yet as the programs were being implemented, a series of comprehensive administrative reforms were being implemented. On a purely administrative level, management techniques such as the creation of a management organization unit were introduced to improve managerial capabilities of the regions and ministries. As for decentralization, in 1994, elections were held for the first time at the prefectoral level, so prefects were no longer state appointees; as we see in the next chapter, this created interesting tensions between the second and third tiers. More importantly, in 1994, the implementation of Laws 2218 and 2240 represented significant steps towards making the *perifereia* a proper level of state administration. Implementation required the co-operation of many authorities, which varied, depending on the subprogram and measure in question.

So there was evidence of Europeanization in the actors and in the reformed administrative structures. The administration appeared to be improving; personnel were better qualified, adopting different modes of operation, and acquiring experience in implementing programs. At the centre, officials in the ministries were slowly giving up their hegemony and accepting the need for sub national input in structural programs, with the result that sub-national actors were emerging as assets. Hence, they were accepting the need for decentralization. Central administrators were also gaining a respect and appreciation for studies and planning, so figures themselves were not the sole criteria for measuring performance. Approaching the problem from the periphery, the *learning* in this instance involved the actors acquiring experience with structural programs, acquiring an appreciation for studies and new techniques, and finding their role vis-à-vis the centre. This also required a re-evaluation of the practice of clientelism. Sub-national actors were accepting the fact that scattering funds for small-scale works was not conducive to effective regional development. These preliminary conclusions are further tested in the chapter that follows.

Appendix A: CSF 1989–1993 Greece*

Five Sub-Programs

Sub-Program ERDF

Improvement of Infrastructures
Measure A1.1   Roads
Measure A1.2   Harbours
Measure A1.3   Airports
Measure A1.6   Children – day-care centres
Measure A1.7   Water supply
Measure A1.9   Protection of the environment

Sub-Program ESF

Measure B.1   Primary sector
Measure B.2   Secondary sector
Measure B.3   Tertiary sector
Measure B.4   Local development

Sub-Program EAGG-F

Measure 1 …
Measure 3   Forest work

Local Self-Administration (EAPTA)

Measure D1   Road construction

Measure D2	Water supply and drainage
Measure D3	Cultural – social armament
Measure D4	Protection of the environment
Measure D5	Tourism
Measure D6	Improvement of the competitiveness of business …

Sub-Program: Implementation (EFARMOGI)

Measure E1	Support – monitoring and projection of the Operational Programs
Measure E2	Support – programs and the formation of the ESF

* The PEPs for both Central Macedonia and West Greece have the same headings.

Appendix B: CSF 1994–1999 Central Macedonia

Sub-Program 1: Empowerment of the New Role of the *Perifereia* and the Metropolitan Role of Thessaloniki

Measure 1   Intervention in the transport sector
Measure 2   Harbour of Thessaloniki
Measure 3   Tertiary training …
Measure 5   Cultural renewal

Sub-Program 2: Support of Competitiveness of Industry

Measure 1   Increase in the competitiveness of MME (small and medium-sized) and new financing means

Sub-Program 3: Improvement in Basic Substructures of City Centres and Quality of life

Measure 1   Improvement in transport substructures
Measure 2   Increase the quality of the substructures of health and welfare
Measure 5   Improvement of tourist areas

Sub-Program 4: Agricultural Development

Measure 1   Land improvement
Measure 2   Animal capital
Measure 5   Forests
Measure 6   Agricultural local development (EGTPE-P)

Measure 7   Improvement of mild forms of energy
Measure 9   Agricultural substructures of local development (ETPA)
Measure 10   Preparation

Sub-Program 5: Improvement in Human Capital

Measure 1   Substructure and equipment training
Measure 2   Continuing vocational equipment for the fight against
             unemployment ...

**Sub-Program 6: Strengthening of Structures
of Local Self-Administration**

Measure 1   Basic infrastructure
Measure 2   Improvement in the quality of life
Measure 3   Support of local economy and productive investments

**Sub-Program 7: Supplement of Functioning of Traits
of PEP 1989–1993**

Sub-Program 8: Application/Enforcement

Sub-Program 9: Local Occupation 1999

Appendix C: CSF 1994–1999 West Greece

Sub-Program 1: West Greece – Gate of Connection with Europe

Measure 1   Basic substructures
Measure 2   Human workforce
Measure 3   Substructure of service for passengers and goods
Measure 4   Supplementary works
Measure 5   Professional organization

Sub-Program 2: Improvement of Quality of Life and Environment

Measure 1   Protection of the environment – water supply, drainage, biological purification
Measure 2   Health and welfare
Measure 3   Culture and tourism …

Sub-Program 3: Development

Measure 1   Land improvement
Measure 2   Improvement of rural substructure
Measure 3   Improvement of mild forms of energy
Measure 4   Agrotourism
Measure 5   Vital production
Measure 6   Forests
Measure 7   Fisheries
Measure 8   Organization

Sub-Program 4: Human Resources

Measure 1   Original formation (substructure second-level training)
Measure 2   Continued arrangement for the fight against unemployment ...

Sub-Program 5: Industrial-Productive Zones

Measure 1   Productive investments
Measure 2   Support of services of the MME
Measure 3   Improvement of the substructure

Sub-Program 6: Support Structure of Local Self-administration

Measure 1   Basic substructure
Measure 2   Environment
Measure 3   Reinforcement support of local self-administration

Sub-Program 7: Completion of Incomplete Projects under CSF (1989–1993)

Sub-Program 8: Application

4 Political Adaptation and Centre–Periphery Politics

Introduction

Considering past failures to reform the political system, and the distinction between legislative provision and practice, it was important to obtain a deeper understanding of how the system was functioning. This chapter offers an in-depth normative test. If the hypotheses were confirmed, then results would indicate that the legal state (*nomimotis*) approximates the real state (*pragmatikotis*), and reforms would not be 'empty shells.'

Interviews were conducted to determine the extent to which central actors perceived a need for real change and the degree to which ideas of decentralization were becoming entrenched in Greek politics. The comments of interviewees helped reveal the reasoning behind the reforms and the results. Interviews were also key in establishing the extent to which sub-national actors were gaining a voice and adopting new levels of cooperation so that they could take advantage of the new opportunities to effect real change. Data from interviews would establish if there was a parallel change in ideology among players and if there were new ways of thinking at both national and sub-national levels. It can be argued that a great deal of what was asked required a self-assessment by civil servants and political elite. That is, the interviewees may have answered in a mechanical way and provided the expected answers. While this may be true, the findings from the interviews were not taken at face value. How the respondents rationalized their answers was carefully scrutinized; it is one thing to 'mechanically' quote the virtues of decentralization, while it is quite another to believably explain why one supports it. Additionally, findings of what officials at one level stated were tested against responses at other levels. So the responses of officials in Greece were cross-checked with responses of Commission officials who had observed the Greek administration. Responses of central elites were tested with responses of sub-national elites. And finally, responses of officials in each of the two sub-national tiers of this study were cross-checked with responses of officials in the other sub-national tier and at the centre. Findings suggest that Europeanization had acquired momentum, involving modernization and reform that was different from that of the past – not an attempt at metamorphosis, but a cultural and political adjustment (interviews with senior officials). The tentative conclusion is that the method of interaction in policy networks related to EU structural policy exhibited characteristics of a Mediterranean regime.

Explaining Reform

Point of Impact

Reforms were placed in a historical context to help establish at what point the EU structural programs had a real effect on the Greek actors. Andrikopoulou and Kafkalas (2004) maintain that new institutional structures introduced during the first half of the 1980s were not tied to Europeanization, but rather should be seen as reforms based on anti-European rhetoric.[1] Similarly, Ioakimidis (1996) suggests that the European Community did not play a role in the development of Law 1622/1986, because the Community did not have a coherent regional policy prior to 1988; PASOK was Euro-sceptic at the time; and Law 1622 makes no reference to the Community. Further, one could argue that this decentralization was simply the realization of PASOK's pre-electoral promises. Finally, the law entrusted regional councils with seven functions, but it does not refer to the design or the implementation of Community policies.

Assuming a middle position, the argument made here is that effects of Europeanization were negligible for two reasons: using the terminology of Andrikopoulou and Kafkalas (2004), the country was in mode two (Euro-sceptic), and regional policy was neither comprehensive nor intrusive enough to warrant pressure for reform. What limited reform did take place, however, can be linked to the IMPs. Problems encountered with the IMPs provided an impetus for Greece to establish a level of regional administration. The IMPs necessitated a level of regional administration, and their successors, the Operational Programs of the first and second CSF, have been the direct cause of the establishment of regional institutions. Although less comprehensive in comparison to the RDPs, the IMPs were nevertheless regional funds (Papageorgiou and Verney 1992; Verney 1994). Further, the initial responsibility of the *perifereies* was the monitoring of Community regional programs. Also, unlike the prefectoral element of Law 1622, the regional aspect of this legislation as it applied to the third tier of decentralization, was partially carried through. This points to a connection to regional programs. As noted earlier, elections at the prefectoral level were not a response to integration; rather, they were partly a response to the political promises of PASOK, and to the general decentralization taking place across much of Europe (Spanou 1998). The *perifereia*, however, was a different matter. The regional aspect of Law 1622 was operationalized because of the regional programs. Getimis and Demetropoulou (2004) argue that – although it was not until the 1990s that Greece fully adjusted its thinking and made a 'full pro-European turn' and 'within the context of the CSF' implemented the necessary reforms – the impact can be traced to Law 1622/1986.

Impact

While the point of impact may be debatable, it can be argued that the Community played a key role in 'encouraging' the PASOK party to introduce regional reforms after 1994 (Featherstone and Yannopoulos 1995; Verney 1994). It can also be argued that as EC structural funds became more comprehensive, qualitatively and quantitatively, there was a corresponding increased attempt to decentralize. Further, it can be argued that, over time, the political philosophy of partnership and subsidiarity 'challenged centralization' (Featherstone and Yannopoulos). The changes represented a significant step towards decentralization and provide 'a good example of institutional reform being encouraged by Brussels, rather than emerging exclusively as the outgrowth of internal political process' (Papageorgiou and Verney 1992, 141; Plaskovitis 1994; Verney 1994). So the structural funds were catalysts for the creation of a plethora of new institutions at the sub-national level; while initially a case of misfit, over time the structural funds have also been an opportunity for institution-building and network creation (Paraskevopoulos 2001). The Greek central administration had been 'forced' to formulate policy within a coherent set of program objectives, and more importantly, it had been asked to share this responsibility with sub-national authorities (Ioakimidis 1994). Evidence also suggested that EC policies create an *internal* pressure for greater administrative decentralization to promote democracy and efficiency (Featherstone and Yannopoulos). This movement is of great significance, because external pressure alone cannot ensure Europeanization and consequently cannot translate into meaningful reforms. Establishing the impetus behind the reforms may help determine how the reforms will function. That is, in order for reforms to take root, there must be an internal consensus for a need to change. As a number of respondents succinctly stated, 'Greeks do not like to be told what to do.'

Having said this, it is interesting that in the period that can be labelled Euro-philic, there was a discrepancy between support for European integration and resistance of successive governments to remove negative aspects of the Greek political system. Research revealed the presence of both an 'old' and 'new' elite. The former involved a minority of individuals who were traditionalist and unenthusiastic about Europe, trying to keep the political system as it was – centralized and clientelist. The latter group comprises modernizing elites who have an interest in Europe. They are a modernizing faction who have participated in policymaking in Brussels, have interacted with Commission officials, and are embracing new ways of thinking. So they use EU membership to decentralize and modernize Greek politics. It should be noted that in Greece, Europeanization is often related to modernization (Featherstone 2005; Paraskevopoulos 2005; Paraskevopoulos and Leonardi 2004; Tsarouhas 2008). Indeed, Prime Minister Simitis's mantras were 'modernization' and 'Europeanization' and were considered synonymous for Greece (Featherstone 2005). His pro-European team included Theodoros Pangalos, Vasso Papandreou, and Georgios Papandreou, whose agenda 'was defined within the context of "Europe": it had little meaning without reference to the need to adapt to the EU: the latter defined and legitimized their project' (Featherstone 2005, 227). The fact that Simitis's agenda was placed within a European context indicates the relevance of Europeanization: 'Simitis' ... identification of the external imperative, his stress on a certain time frame affecting choice, and his interpretation of how EU pressures and domestic needs are to be made compatible are all crucial to an understanding of his mission' (232).

Findings from interviews support the above. Senior civil servants in the central ministries and sub-national actors gave a two-fold answer to the question of why reforms were initiated. The first reason was that it was time and that change is part of the country's wider *sintagma* (goal), and the second was that the EU structural funds in particular acted as a force for change. The 'reasons for reform are complicated, but EU programs represent one, if not the main force' (interview with upper-level civil servants within the Ministry of the Interior). While reforms may have eventually taken place in the absence of EU membership, the 'EU drove the current reforms and penetrated them' (ibid.). The argument can be made that officials were merely dictating an official line, but their response was taken at face value because there was no apparent need for them to lie and connect the reforms to the EU. Further, evidence shows that there was real devolution and movement towards real partnership. However, a difference in the order of response and in emphasis is noteworthy. Retrospective analysis of what created the change was often subjective and partly a matter of Greek pride; the answer 'it is time' is more suggestive of an independent initiative to change. Since Greeks do not want to be told what to do, in order for them to change, they must *want* to. Doing what one wants is more productive than doing what should be done. In other words, a case of misfit alone does not ensure change.

A senior civil servant who was on the team that framed the decentralization laws of the 1990s noted, 'The Greek administration was being pushed by the Commission, but Greek officials also saw a need for reform.' Officials realized that not everything could be controlled by the centre (interviews with senior officials in the Ministry of the Interior). Although some officials in the central ministries did not want to devolve responsibility and lose powers, there was a greater consensus than in the past of a need to carry out some type of decentralization (interviews with MNE and Ministry of the Interior). Central ministries did not have a clear understanding of what was happening in the regions; decentralization was needed because 'only regional actors know the region's needs.' Regional authorities bring a practical experience to policymaking, which is much needed when framing and implementing regional programs (interviews with officials in MNE). Interviewees noted that 'times are changing and the *anagkes* [needs] are changing.' The *anagky* (need) equals membership of the EU (interviews with upper-level civil servant in Central Macedonia, West Greece; interviews with senior officials in the Ministry of the Interior; interviews with officials in the MNE).

Effects on the Three Strands: The Evolving Politics

Devolution assumed administrative and political guises. Administrative reform entailed establishing institutions in the periphery and staffing them. The aim of this review was to establish who was placed in the sub-national institutions and how the administration was functioning. With respect to decentralization, it was necessary to further establish whether or not real powers had been allocated to the sub-national levels. Further, there was also the question of how politics was being played out in relations between actors at national and sub-national levels, and among the sub-national actors themselves.

Clientelism

The significance of clientelism in Greek politics has been established; the argument is that clientelism has both a cultural and a structural explanation in Greece. It may be only one strand of the Greek political system, but this strand runs through the second strand, the administration, and the third, the centre periphery nexus. Although this study did not produce drastic results, evidence does suggest that the practice of clientelism had altered.

Part of the explanation of the change in the practice of clientelism can be found in the movement of new political and intellectual elites to the first and second levels of local government and particularly to the *perifereies*. In the prefectoral and municipal elections of October 1998, professors, lawyers, and members of Parliament became candidates for prefects and mayors and were even vying for a seat in council.[2] So new actors were moving to the periphery. On the one hand, the attraction of the sub-national arena can be explained by the shift in power and by the subsequent attraction of sub-national political arenas. As sub-national tiers gain powers at the expense of MP's, the shift in powers to the periphery offers a new arena in which to capture power. There are also higher salaries and fringe benefits. On the other hand, since the introduction of the Law of *Peponi*, members of Parliament lost their 'rousfeti card' at this level. The Ministry of the Interior noted that 'the ministries have lost their powers to hire: they must be cut off from every form of clientelist connections and devote their time to strategic politics' (*Kathimerini*, 4 October 1998).

A cynical explanation stresses the increased funding available to local authorities, and hence a greater opportunity to provide further political favours at the sub-national level. If clientelism shifts to the periphery, structural funds can become a source for supporting patronage systems at the sub-national level. It is noted below that a few upper-level civil servants did mention that there were still attempts to branch out projects so that they could satisfy patronage obligations. But many political and administrative individuals represent a new elite intent on modernizing Greek politics and on curbing the practice of clientelism. Although it takes time for institutional changes to influence political culture and practice, since the *anagkes* are changing, in time, the *nootropia* (way of thinking) will also change (interviews with upper-level central civil servants). While clientelism has not disappeared, it has adjusted. Further, there is an interesting safeguard incorporated into the new model vis-à-vis the regional secretaries, who are political appointees. On the one hand, clientelism is strong, as it is projected in the mediation role of the regional secretary. But these same secretaries have been assigned the *eleghitiko rolo* (monitoring role) so that the practice of clientelism at the prefectoral level is constantly scrutinized. Regional secretaries try to keep clientelism under control and help transform it, so that long-term, comprehensive regional development and electoral success are not seen as incompatible (interviews with central and regional officials).

The Administration

Spanou (1998) advocates a pluralistic approach when studying administrative systems of EU member states, which acknowledges co-existing models of varying weight, influence, and capacity for implementation within the EU; varying similarities and dissimilarities; and both formal and informal aspects. Distance from one type of model does not indicate a lack of development (Spanou). The goal in this study was not to identify or establish a specific Greek administrative paradigm. To have laboured with that intent might have been unrealistic, considering the complexity of administrative systems – after all, administration can be a nebulous concept – and it would not have been useful for this book's purposes. Instead, this work attempts to identify the elements which are being weaved into the existing administrative model.

The 'pluralist approach' to studying administrative systems is of particular importance in cases such as Greece, where there is a gap between formal rules and informal practices. It is also very appropriate in understanding the general climate and approach of the Greek reforms. Indeed, perhaps the most significant aspect of the reforms was the change in approach. The aim was not to copy the system of any one country, but to do what works for Greece, even if this means establishing a model that is different from that of any other EU member state. Further, officials in the Ministry of the Interior argued that the Greek administration does not need a metamorphosis, but rather a *metarrithmisi* (reformation). This rationale assisted reform, permitting retention of elements that were beneficial and abandonment of those that were not.

Although there is no evidence that a specific model was followed, there is some connection with new public management (NPM) theory, which embraces privatization, contracting out, consumerism, and bottom-up policymaking. NPM is evident in the use of private managers in implementing structural programs, borrowing from NPM notions that the public sector can benefit by contracting out to the private sector. It is also evident in the incorporation of the principle of subsidiarity. Indeed, it is argued below that subsidiarity is being adopted by the Greek political system. Further, administrative devolution that is focused on the *perifereia* adopts language similar to that of NPM in that the legislation provides that the centre will 'steer' and guide, while the periphery will implement. Reforms involve a 'harmonization' of tools and institutions that has not been used before. 'accountability' through evaluation; partnership; and most importantly, the EU *structural programs* (interviews with officials in the Commission, regional administrations, and the central administration). There is a strong connection between the EU structural funds and the administrative reforms (officials in central administration; Commission officials). Experience from past periods provides evidence that the public administration plays a significant role in how structural policy is implemented (interviews with central officials in the MNE). The Regional Operational Programs are comprehensive programs, with a clear time frame, monetary-economic and natural goals that require clear methods of operation and rational management. What was needed was a transgression of the system, and that was attained with the introduction of a multi-layered authority that is released from the classical hierarchy of the administration and hence able to operate productively, efficiently, and flexibly.

To begin, there appears to be a belief that if one engages qualified personnel, the model is less important, so stress is placed on acquiring experienced, qualified personnel (interviews with Ministry of the Interior), and that requires an attack on the practice of bureaucratic clientelism (interviews with upper-level civil servants in Ministry of the

Interior). In regional administration, clientelism as a method of appointment is being eroded, albeit slowly (interviews with upper-level civil servants), and while the practice of using social criteria has not disappeared, it is decreasing (interviews with officials in both regional and central administrations). Interviews provided evidence of movement towards more objective hiring where qualifications took priority over such factors as marital status and number of children. More importantly, there was an increasing awareness that proper training and experience were needed for efficiency and effectiveness in one's post.[3] Administration of the structural programs required experts and specialists who could undertake the necessary studies, plan and analyse, and offer novel ideas (interviews within the MNE and Ministry of the Interior, with upper-level officials from regions, and with Commission officials). Technical experts were engaged to monitor the programs, consider implementation, and measure the results, so that any necessary adjustments can be made. Since the Greek administration had little experience in dealing with such matters, it often relied on outside expertise when developing, implementing, and evaluating structural programs. So in the later 1990s, there was an increase in contracting out, but this was not necessarily problematic because it assisted the administration in its *learning*, and it can be more efficient to contract a service.

Further, the hiring of personnel for the public sector was at a developed stage and significant efforts were being taken to address the administrative shortcomings of sub-national administrations (interview with upper-level civil servants in the Ministry of the Interior). But some individuals do not want to leave Athens to go to the *perifereies*.[4] In comparison to other *perifereies*, Central Macedonia had better trained personnel because civil servants were transferred from the Ministry of Macedonia and Thrace, which was located in Thessaloniki (interviews, upper-level civil servant in the Ministry of the Interior).[5] Consequently, Central Macedonia was advancing the best of the thirteen *perifereies* (interview, upper-level civil servant in the Ministry of the Interior). Further, the prefectoral administrations were lagging behind the *perifereies* in reform. Problems arose because the primary personnel of the prefectures were composed of detachments from the former prefectures. These civil servants often continued to function with the same frame of mind and procedures that they used in the past, not realizing that they constituted a part of the independent prefecture (interview with prefect of Thessaloniki; Papadopoulos 1997). So time was needed for prefectoral actors to become accustomed to the new administrative reality. Thus, Europeanization was not as strong here.

Formal integration is only one element of reform. Much more was happening informally and is more difficult to identify (Spanou 1998). The end is dependent on pre-existing patterns of functioning, as well as on constraints implied by EU membership and the need to deliver specific results. Evidence supports Spanou's argument that 'for Greece, the process of integration in administrative terms corresponds to an attempt to bridge the gap between formal rules and informal practices' (481). Civil servants in the *perifereies* admitted this, one going as far as to say that there are days when the office is in a state of chaos. But this is not a negative aspect of the reforms; rather, it is further evidence of *learning* and *Europeanization*. Indeed, it can also be argued that decision-makers learn many lessons in how to improve their interventions and 'this *learning* process is not always formally structured' (European Commission 1999b).

Overall, reform was considered a 'continuous and long-term process because it takes time for civil servants to adjust' (interview with officials in the Ministry of the Interior). Respondents noted that what should be stressed is the change in the administration (interviews with upper-level civil servants and political elites). Administrative personnel had improved and continued to improve. Spanou (1998) concluded that the 'dynamics of transition are perceptible' and that the EU started to change the conditions under which the Greek political administration operates. Although more research is needed to determine whether or not this is expanding to other policy areas, in the context of structural funds, individuals in the Commission have seen a transformation in the administration. There were civil engineers, economists, and other experts engaged in the process. There was also a change in the way the administration was operating. It is interesting that Commission officials who participated in monitoring committees were Greek, but they were judging how their counterparts in the Greek administration in Greece were performing. It appears that Greek officials in the Commission have adopted the Commission's methods of operation. This may be further evidence of a *learning* and *Europeanization* that comes from years of interaction with officials from other EU member states and from experience with the structural programs themselves. Civil servants, politicians, and academics all stressed that 'everyone is learning.' There was also an understanding of a need to improve efficiency. In the past, the *stochos* (goal) was to obtain project approvals, but over time, authorities became less concerned with simply obtaining funds. So the Commission was not alone in pushing for these procedures (interview with Plaskovitis, with officials in the MNE, and with Commission officials). The advantages of securing administrative capacity was important in itself. It can be argued that the administrative culture is now changing and that officials at all administrative levels perceive process, studies, analysis, and cooperation as important. Indeed, political and administrative officials encourage collaboration between many levels of actors and between private and public actors (interviews with civil servants in the *perifereies* and with officials in the Ministry of the Interior). The *anagki*, as noted above, is EU membership.

The Centre–Periphery Nexus: Understanding the Greek Elites

The Logic of the Centre

Regionalization was a top-down response to the changing demands on the political system. Central elites argued that development must be from the bottom up and that there must be respect for the principle of subsidiarity (interviews with upper-level civil servants). The new rationale argument was that one can *kiverna* (govern) from afar, but one cannot *dioikei* (administer).

The result is that the *perifereies* are administrative units, but they are rather independent of the state. Each *perifereia* exercises its power through its civil service within its geographical area, including civil servants within the prefecture. Powers are moving to the *perifereia*, but the state has also moved to the *perifereia* (interviews with central ministries). That is, the responsibility given to the regional council to decide is quasi-political, because representatives from the first and second tiers are elected in their respective jurisdictions, while the tasks of the decentralized ministries to implement are purely administrative. The *perifereia* gains more than its previous programming role; it has the power to implement national and regional plans. It is a new administrative unit that can program, design, coordinate, and apply the policies of economic, social, and political development. Central actors argue that it unifies the dispersed cross-prefectoral offices of the ministries into a new organization to improve coordination and programming. So it becomes a framework for the effective exercise of the powers transferred from the central administration, securing unhindered and productive cooperation with the central administration for national programming. It is the *syndetico kriko* (connecting link) bridging the central administration and self-governance (Ministry of the Interior, Local Governance, and Decentralization 1997; interviews with central administration). Interviews with top civil servants in the MNE indicated that they considered sub-national input necessary for a comprehensive and effective structural policy. At the sub-national level, officials supported these claims, noting that in the last few years, the MNE played a less dominant, more cooperative role. Examination of the two programming periods (1989–93, 1994–9) shows an increased respect for – and weight placed on – the opinions of sub-national actors. Central authorities realized and accepted the fact that sub-national officials are needed for policy to be effective. The centre adopts a 'strategic role of development' (interviews with senior officials at the centre). It establishes the ends it wants to achieve and enables the decentralized authorities to implement these policies.

Again, one can question whether respondents were simply quoting 'official lines.' But their statements are not difficult to believe. The central administration was accepting the need for administrative devolution to secure a level of administration that could address regional policies and adapt and implement central regulations as it deemed appropriate. Further, it is administrative devolution that was being stressed. The focus on the *perifereia* is interesting and warrants further elaboration. The regional tier is seen as a more appropriate level for dealing with regional issues (interviews with officials at central and sub-national levels; EU Commission), but the *perifereia* poses a lesser threat to central powers than do the elected prefectures do. This is where *ta politica* were expected to have a decisive role. Accepting decentralization was the first step to reform, and the second is actual implementation. The question was how the new administration was functioning and how they were using their new powers: how were the actors playing the game?

Sub-National Elites: Europeanization in the Periphery

From the late 1980s, partnership with the EU became an attractive prospect for prefectoral elites (Papageorgiou and Verney 1992). They were even aware of the need to establish an identity within the EC, and some wanted direct links with Brussels (Papageorgiou and Verney). Most prefectoral actors at the time, however, looked to Athens for guidance, information, and contacts with the EC. Further, there was overwhelming support for decentralization among the councillors, who wanted more power over cultural affairs, taxes for local projects, environment, agriculture, health, public works, employment, and industrial development, to name a few (Verney and Papageorgiou 1992). This view is not surprising, considering that many of the prefectoral councillors represented an upwardly mobile, well-educated, and relatively young elite (Verney and Papageorgiou).[6] So they were a prime group for reform and Europeanization.

Direct elections of the prefectoral councils, though not a result of Europeanization, were an important step for it. The fact that the prefect was now a native of the region could help him or her better identify with the region. It could also help the prefect's relationship with the people, since he or she was referred to as 'one of us' (interviews with officials in the prefectures). Evidence suggests that prefectoral actors were unsatisfied with the changes. At the time of this study, the prefect of Thessaloniki had had a long career in local politics as a municipal councillor since 1975. He supported European integration, noting that the EU in general, and structural funds in particular, played a major role in the decentralizing reforms. He had forged links with the Commission and wanted them to deepen. The prefect of Achaia was also pro-Europe, noting that the EU membership was beneficial – Greece belonged to Europe and needed Europe. The two prefects considered EU programs important resources for their regions' development, so they had a vested interest in the proper implementation of the funds and in reform.

Ta Politica: Relations between Elites

Elections might have taken place in the prefectures, but not much came of it (interviews with Ministry of the Interior). Indeed, the prefect was losing power while the regional secretary was gaining power. Most interviewees argued that the regional secretary was gaining the power of the prefecture, representing the state (interviews with upper-level civil servants in the Ministry of the Interior, and with Commission officials).

The role and views of the regional secretary – the novel actor in this game – were very interesting. At the time of this research, the regional secretary of West Greece supported many of the ideas of modernization and decentralization. He was satisfied with decentralization and the role that the *perifereia* was acquiring and was in no hurry to secure greater devolution. He stated that the *perifereia* must first secure functioning regional administrations and clear responsibilities for each level. Further, he stressed that people needed time to become accustomed to the idea of the *perifereia*. And he argued that in the near future the role of the regional secretary should be that of minister of the region. However, regional secretaries do not like the centre 'hovering' above their heads, and this resistance creates tension (interviews with Commission officials and with senior officials in the Ministry of the Interior). This may be one explanation as to why the regional secretary wanted to be a minister: a minister would have more powers and less supervision from the central administration. Politics, however, had entered the picture, manifested in the relations between the second- and the third-tier elites, and to a lesser extent between the third tier and the centre.

Two types of tensions were revealed: one resulting from a clash between the new and old elite, and the second from a power struggle between the second and third tiers. The explanation for the former was that the regional secretary supervised/monitored the clientelist practices of the prefectures. The explanation for the latter was that prefects believed that because they were elected, power should go to them under the rules of subsidiarity. The findings outlined below are quite interesting.

Tension between Old and New Elite

The established prefecture was to a certain extent more traditional, while the regional actors at the *perifereies* represented a modernizing elite. Although it was noted above that both prefects supported EU membership, their approach towards the *politica* was different when compared to that of the elites of the *perifereies*. Their administrations evoked a sense of the old-school mayor. Further, the regional secretary, officials in the Ministry of the Interior, and the Commission all maintained that clientelism was still present at the prefectoral level. The regional group of sub-national actors was largely representative of a new generation committed to Europe; they will be instruments for Europeanization. The *perifereies* were staffed with new civil servants, many of whom held university degrees. This group has an incentive to further the economic development of the region (and regional firms) so that they can compete in the internal market. Since these actors are from the new elite, they can be expected to tap into inherent strengths of the region and address its weaknesses. They have a specific interest in proper implementation of structural funds and a general interest in modernization of Greek politics. They have witnessed how Commission officials operate and have come to question traditional methods of operation (interviews with officials in both regions, and with Commission officials).

Indeed, the regional secretary assumes the role of gatekeeper of *rousfeti*. It is interesting that a political appointee has been assigned to keep clientelism in check. The regional secretary of West Greece viewed his role as ensuring that the prefect does not do everything he wishes. That is, the regional secretary tried to keep political favours in check and to look at things objectively. Unlike the prefect, the regional secretary has no reason to grant political favours (interview with regional secretary and with Commission officials). This is not to argue that if the regional secretary were elected he would retreat to old forms of clientelism. Rather, his point was that all politicians are concerned with re-election and hence seek to satisfy the broader electorate. He noted that prefects had a tendency to consider smaller projects, which offer more immediate rewards. He was able to play a stricter role in curbing clientelist practices because he was unburdened with such preoccupations. It was noted that problems arise when prefects try to enter into areas where they shouldn't, and where they have no responsibility (interviews with officials in regional offices). In one example, the central administration wanted to erect a building, but the prefect wanted to get a project that pleased the broader electorate, with the result that the prefect agreed to the project but attempted to attach irrigation to the expenses.

It is difficult to say with certainty how the system functioned. The prefects were experienced, so they knew their political arena, but they were better trained at the *perifereia*, and many of these administrators do not allow clientelism to prevail. The gate-keeping role, however, appeared to be working well. Clientelism as 'attachment' decreased between the first (1989–93) and the second (1994–9) programming period. Again, more research is needed, but it was estimated that this happens in 25 to 30 per cent of overall programs (interviews with regional officials).

Tensions Resulting from Power Struggles

It was hardly surprising that the regional secretary's supervisory role over the prefectures created problems: 'The prefect does not want anyone over his or her head' (interviews with central administration and

Commission officials). Getimis and Demetropoulou (2004) argue that there is a suspicion among local actors, who consider the regional secretariat another state bureaucratic entity threatening their existence; and they are aware that regional actors started from scratch and lacked knowledge and experience. Central civil servants noted the strain between regional secretaries and prefects that occurred across all *perifereies*, so an expression of harmonious relations with their respective regional secretaries by the prefects of Thessaloniki and Achaia was surprising. Although it was not expected that the prefects would admit to tensions resulting from clientelist practices that the regional secretary sought to curb, it was surprising that they were reluctant to admit to any strains. It was even more surprising, considering that in several papers the prefect of Thessaloniki had expressed his frustrations at the lack of powers of the prefectures. When probed a little further, however, both prefects did note certain difficulties. They argued that in order to operate in the system of EU policymaking, they needed constitutional status and economic resources, so they were determined to retain their newly acquired areas of responsibility. They referred to decentralization in other member states, noting that modernization is decentralization with strong self-government. They stressed that powers should be divided among the three sub-national tiers so that the principle of *epikourikotita* (subsidiarity) is respected.

The fact that the principle of subsidiarity was being adopted in the political dialogue of Greek actors is evidence of an intellectual diffusion resulting from EU interaction; it was being used by actors at all political levels – central, regional, and prefectoral – as they attempted to claim powers. This Europeanization is significant, considering that the principle was a concept foreign to Greek politics. Both prefects' definitions of subsidiarity stressed a bottom-up rather than cooperative policymaking. They noted that powers of the prefecture must be secured before further changes are made to the *perifereies*. There was the danger that the centre was trying to capture powers from the prefect – a danger of turning the regional secretary into the old prefect (interview with prefect of Thessaloniki). The prefect of Thessaloniki noted that there was also a danger the central administration was reintroducing the centralizing state at the level of the *perifereia* (Papadopoulos 1997). He further stressed that 'the significant resources that the *perifereia* manages confirm and reproduce the existing model. They do not reform; rather, they decentralize the same structures, reproducing its *pathogenia* [affliction]' (ibid.). On the other hand, prefects also argued that establishment of the *perifereia* was beneficial because they did not have to go to Athens – 'Athens' was there, so problems were resolved more quickly and more efficiently. But prefects used whatever relay they could: the regional secretary, the ministries, and the Commission. There is evidence that they intervene for the good of their prefecture and pressurize their regional secretary. One example cited was the highway that joins Thessaloniki and Kalamata; Patra also wanted to be in this route and wanted a Patra–Athens highway, so they pressured the regional secretary who in turn acted on their behalf vis-à-vis the central administration. Sometimes prefects go directly to the centre. They claimed that on occasion this was quicker than taking the regional route. There was also a fear among some prefects that the regional secretary would favour one prefecture over another (interview with Ministry of the Interior), so going directly to the centre was an option when they were dissatisfied with the results they achieved with the regional secretary.

Resolution of Tension: Europeanization as Manifested in Mediterranean Regimes

One way to approach the question of cooperation was to try to establish the quality of relations between the prefect and the mayor prior to 1994 – before direct elections of the prefectoral councils. The argument can be made that as long as the careers of the regional administrators depended on obedience to the centre, regional interests would not be satisfied (Featherstone and Yannopoulos 1994; Verney and Papageorgiou 1992). A central control of the periphery was, however, inconclusive. It is true that as long as the careers of the prefects were dependent upon the centre, their loyalties remained divided: prefects were forced to follow the orders of the Ministry of the Interior so they could not stray far from the orders of the centre, but they had a responsibility to assist local politicians and were dependent upon the local elite to implement central legislation. This meant that cooperation would be more effective than a top-down attempt to control. The relationship between prefect and local elites has not been studied extensively in Greece. The assumption here was that within the centralized Greek state, there are power relationships between central and peripheral political elites similar to those Grémion (1976) found in France. The prefect of Achaia noted that in before 1994 period, the prefect was in control, but good relations were needed for things to run smoothly. This, he said, was understood by all. Indeed, if there was no cooperation, the centre could not get its policies implemented (interviews with sub-national officials and at the Ministry of the Interior).

Evidence points to a more complicated version of *symbiosis* between the regional secretary and prefect after 1994. Although tension results from the frustrations that prefects face, officials noted that actors were able to put power struggles aside in order to enter the game. If we consider the problem from below, a voice within the regional council and monitoring committee is better than no voice at all. And from above, the central administration was increasingly valuing the input of sub-national actors. So the stress is on building a consensus to secure common interests (interviews with national, sub-national, and Commission officials). It is not always a question of whether the prefecture or the *perifereia* has jurisdiction; rather, it is what they can do to ensure an effective program to secure EU funding. Indeed, there is seldom a defined separation of responsibility in implementation of EU regional programs. Development itself was defined as reaching the goal of programs through cooperation and partnership; the emphasis is on consensus of all involved (interviews with officials in MNE, in sub-national administrations, and with Commission officials).

Papageorgiou and Verney (1992) found that the role of the regional secretary was important. When the regional secretary took an active interest in the formulation of the RDP and exercised the right to hold regional conferences and information meetings, the result was much closer to an integrated plan than was the case with the IMPs. This potential role of the regional secretary was commented on during the interviews conducted in West Greece. The regional secretary takes on the role of mediator and speaks on behalf of the prefecture as well. Everyone has a voice through the regional secretary. For example, even representatives from the MNE discussed issues with the regional secretary, and the regional secretary in turn spoke on their behalf during meetings of the monitoring committees (Commission officials). However, the role of the regional secretary is not that of the prefect of the past. There are more actors involved, and the policy process has become more integrated. On the one hand, since the regional secretary is a political appointee, his or her presence may be a means to curb sub-national actors at the prefectoral level. Indeed, some central officials indicated that the regional secretary was a means for the centre to monitor and perhaps contain some powers that the prefectures had gained in 1994. On the other hand, the locus of decision-making was moving to the *perifereia*, so there was less need for a mediation role than before 1994. Instead of having a need for mediation, there is a more direct participation and cooperation among all three sub-national levels.[7] The regional secretary of West Greece noted that, despite the problems listed above, there are productive relations among the three sub-national tiers.

Evidence from interviews suggests that regional secretaries with experience in local politics know that they must cooperate. Indeed, they cannot antagonize other players. Cooperation and consensus-building between the regional secretary and the prefect is a prerequisite for successful regional development (upper-level civil servants from Central Macedonia and West Greece). From his experience in local politics, the prefect of Thessaloniki knew that he must cooperate and does so (upper-level civil servants in Central Macedonia). Indeed, one explanation for the prefects' initial hesitation to admit to tension outlined above is that they did cooperate overall. Further, if the regional secretary and the prefect are from the same political party, as was the case at the time of this study, there is better cooperation (interview with Commission officials). It was noted that there was dialogue between actors before final meetings of the prefectoral councils and the regional councils. So, in many cases, the meetings were *tipika* (a formality) because agreement had been reached beforehand. Cooperation was also evident in the workings of the regional council.

In the late 1980s, Verney and Papageorgiou (1992) found that 'mediating the conflicting interests of the various groups of the Prefecture' was the second-lowest priority. The authors argued that 'the concept of politics as mediation between different interest groups has not taken root to the same extent as in other West European countries' (124). Although more research is needed, evidence from interviews suggests that this was beginning to change. Actors in the regional councils stressed the importance of reaching consensus and intervening to try to find solutions when the interests of two groups conflict. Indeed, the regional council and the regional monitoring committee, both by-products of the Structural Funds (Getimis and Demetropoulou 2004), are useful for co-operation, networking, and partnerships. In their study of the Southern Aegean Islands, Getimis and Demetropoulou found that the interaction between these actors helped them accept new European practices to reduce clientelism and enabled them find a common ground. Similarly, Lavdas (2005) argues the existence of evolving policy networks, which should be differentiated from traditional clientelistic links.

So evidence suggests that EU influence has encouraged cooperation. The way that 'Brussels' functions is very much attuned with the concept of regime. Although an amalgam of policy styles converge in Brussels, the principle behind the EU's existence is that members believe that, together, they can achieve what individually they cannot. There is fluidity and a cooperative nature to their interaction, particularly so in structural policy. Here Europeanization entails adopting elements of this interaction in the Greek domestic context. The new system is very complex, resting on cooperation among multiple levels of state administrative agencies and governments. Indeed, it can be argued that European integration can encourage the movement of policymaking into networks (Balme and Jouve 1996). In Greece, this network came together at the level of the *perifereia*. Interest groups were perceiving a change in power and lobbied all levels of the administration. This branching out of organized interests may also be because the state realized the importance of the private sector in implementing structural policy. The argument is that in order to succeed, there must be input from all affected authorities. Private-sector actors bring new life and new ideas to the process because they are not as stagnant as the public sector. Further, all actors, including interest groups, tried to resolve any disputes between groups in the councils. Interest-group representatives from the private sector also used whatever relay they could. They lobbied their own prefect and other prefects of their *perifereia* and the regional secretary prior to regional council meetings. Voices were heard as one through decisions in the regional councils and monitoring committees. Further, the regional council was believed to have less influence than the monitoring committee of the CSF. A great deal was happening informally and ad hoc. Central, regional, and prefectoral actors become intermeshed so that the distinction between levels loses importance. Sometimes the *perifereia* has responsibility with the centre, while at other times the centre may pass responsibility to the *perifereia* (interviews with MNE officials involved with the programs since IMPs). So new channels of communication have been opened between the centre and the periphery. Everyone realized the need for cooperation and *symbiosis*. Actors depend on one another for successful regional development. Indeed, cooperation seems to be their only vehicle for succeeding and everyone appeared to be well aware of this. So there was a substantial change in centre–periphery relations. At times, this change was also symbolic and informal, as was the case with the administrative reforms.

This interaction was beginning to resemble a Mediterranean regime. Policies facing the Greek administration are complicated, and this has created an understanding that power relations among players must change. It is not a question of who has power over whom, but whether or not actors can secure their ends. It can also be argued that to the extent that the administration depends upon the cultural setting, some strands of the Greek mode of operation will weave through the reformed model. Indeed, this was the opinion of Commission officials, academics, and officials in the Greek Ministry of the Interior. To the extent that clientelism often involves personalistic, informal relations, its presence in the Greek system is beneficial. It permits actors to work around rules that could act as barriers. The rationale of the centre can be summarized readily: 'We will do whatever is needed to ensure Greece's political and economic success, and since this entails cooperation with sub-national actors, then co-operate we will.'

Conclusions

Evidence from interviews suggests a strong connection between the decentralizing and administrative reforms and the EU structural programs. The administration is improving, as is evident in the sophistication of its plans, the type of research, and the comprehensive approach to regional development (interviews with Commission officials and Greek academics). This reform was initiated by the demands of the structural programs. What is important is that this comprehensive approach was adopted by Greek officials. Change has meant that clientelism was reduced because more emphasis was placed on securing long-term regional development as opposed to short-term clientelist ends. So it can be argued that structural programs have helped constrain clientelism. This is not to argue that clientelism has been abolished. Evidence of such a change was not expected, nor is it likely to change in the near future. Finally, and perhaps most profoundly, centre–periphery relations have been disturbed networks have been destabilized, and there has been a re-evaluation of the functioning of the political system. Indeed, it can be argued that devolution was slowly being reinforced by the emergence of new political elites across all levels who acknowledge the benefits of cooperation. There also appeared to be a real movement towards a tri-level partnership. This is further evidence of a Europeanization where centralization is seen as a vice and where the importance of sub-national actors in implementation is being realized. Movement from the IMPs to the RDPs of the first and second CSF shows that the input and role of the regional authorities increased, as did the weight placed on their opinions (interviews with sub-national actors at second and third tiers, and with Commission officials).

5 A Few Tentative Conclusions

For the purpose of this work, Europeanization has been conceptualized as a process of adjustment that domestic actors perceive as beneficial or necessary. The fact that Greek actors have questioned assumptions about the centre–periphery nexus, the system of administration, and the practice of clientelism is indicative of Europeanization. Their aim was not a complete metamorphosis, but a reform of the system that it is adapted to the Greek context and culture. This is a pragmatic response to the problems plaguing Greek politics, adopting what works and abandoning what does not. Elements of tradition that are part of Greek history and culture are not perceived as contradictory to modernization; rather, they are elements that give Greece its own individuality and character without divorcing it from the rest of Europe (Fatouros 1993). Further, there was emerging an ethnic assertion that was different from that of the 1980s vis-à-vis the outside: 'Yes, we are part of Europe, but we are also Greek.' This is an important aspect of Greece's Europeanization. Being European is a good thing, but being Greek has many advantages. This is a pride focused not on ancient achievements but on Greece's current and future position within Europe.

Effect on the Three Strands

The literature on other EU member states pointed to a connection between structural programs and decentralization. Although it is difficult to argue the existence of a single European administrative model, structural programs do presume decentralized management structures. So there is emphasis on process, and results are dependant upon a well-functioning administration embracing the principle of partnership between levels of administration and public and private actors. Further, institutions are needed to implement programs, to monitor them, and to evaluate performance. So member sates must have administrative capacity at the regional level. Finally, adjustment depends on the degree of policy fit and the domestic response to this fit or misfit.

Problems with the programs provided the impetus for Greek decentralization. There was, however, the question of why it took so long for substantial reform to take place. The hypothesis was that the Greek system was quite flawed and that it required additional time for the effect to take place. If this argument held, then as the EU structural funds became more comprehensive, qualitatively and quantitatively, there would be evidence of a corresponding increased attempt to decentralize.

In the post-1994 period, there is evidence of significant reform. There has been an increased role permitted to sub-national actors, a corresponding increased movement towards administrative devolution has been evident in the established *perifereies*, and there has been improved performance in implementation. Hence, there is evidence of learning on many levels. The administrative schema includes two regional tiers – one administrative, the other political. The thirteen *perifereies* of the third tier became de-concentrated administrations, a new type of regional prefecture. The *perifereies* and the general directorates of the *perifereies* were organized into functioning administrations with their own personnel and their own responsibilities. They were given administrative responsibility, particularly in regional development. There has also been a transfer of powers from the central administration to the thirteen regional administrations. Further, the prefecture of the second tier became a directly elected sub-national government. Prefects, in particular, gained extensive powers and have considerable resources at their disposal. In the post-1997 period, however, the focus began shifting to the *perifereia*. So as the regional tier increased in importance, the prefecture decreased. This shift in emphasis corresponds to a shift in sub-national responsibility for structural funds. That is, prefectoral and regional actors gained access to structural policy through the *regional* council and *regional* monitoring committees. Indeed, the regional council was described as the 'place of expression' of local governments and the representatives of the productive classes.

The institutionalization of a sub-national administration was a significant step towards reform. The next task was to determine how the politics were being played between the centre–periphery and among sub-national actors themselves. One way of doing this was to establish how these relationships operated before 1994, in the period prior to the direct elections of the prefectures. The working hypothesis was that the centre did not have complete control of the periphery and that evidence would uncover relationships between central and sub-national actors similar to those found in France by Grémion (1976). While more research is needed, evidence does suggest there was cooperation between the centre and the periphery. Those interviewed noted that the prefect could not antagonize the mayor because this was not conducive to good policy implementation. Further, it was more productive for mayors to try to get prefects to speak on their behalf and to intervene for the good of the prefecture. This symbiotic relationship is also evident in the current relationship between prefects and regional secretaries. On the one hand, the fact that the *perifereia* was gaining powers at the expense of the prefecture created tension between the second- and third-tier actors. On the other hand, this also created a complicated inter-connectedness between levels because actors realized that if they do not cooperate, they lose the opportunity to participate and to influence policy. Europeanization in this instance involved actors acquiring experience with structural programs, acquiring an appreciation for new techniques, and finding their respective roles vis-à-vis the centre and their sub-national partners. Approaching the problem from above, central actors in the ministries were tentatively giving up their hegemonic role and accepting the need for sub-national input in structural programs. Central actors were also gaining a respect and appreciation for studies and planning, so figures themselves were no longer the sole criteria for measuring performance. Qualitative factors were gaining a new respect when measuring performance. This type of programming results in a more comprehensive regional development, and central actors realized that this requires sub-national input, so sub-national actors are seen as an asset, not as a threat. Indeed, central actors came to accept that sub-national actors bring a practical experience to the policy process that is much needed.

On a purely administrative level, the rationale appears to be that if one employs qualified personnel, the model is of lesser importance, so emphasis is on acquiring experienced and qualified personnel. This required an attack on the practice of bureaucratic clientelism (interviews with upper-level civil servants in the Ministry of the Interior). Evidence does suggest the slow erosion of clientelism as a method of appointment. The practice of using social criteria had hardly disappeared, but it was decreasing; more importantly, there was an increasing awareness that proper training and experience were needed for efficiency and effectiveness in one's post. Sub-national administrations were staffed with qualified civil servants, but there was room for further improvement. Problems arose in enticing individuals to leave Athens for the periphery. Reform also entails changing how the administration performs its function. Placing better-qualified personnel does not guarantee immediate results; time is needed for the administration to gain experience and an appreciation of the importance of studies, analysis, and report writing.

The focus of this study with respect to administration has been confined to the administration as it pertains to EU structural funding. Hence, any findings on improvement are within the confines of this policy in the span of two structural programming periods.[1] Having said this, evidence in the performance of structural programs does point to an improvement in the administration. Movement from the IMPs to the CSF (1994–9) indicates that the Greek programs were becoming more comprehensive. This requires qualified actors to produce well-developed plans. There is also a qualitative improvement in performance, for long term development was taking precedence over the satisfaction of short-term clientelist ends. Although the practice of 'attachments' had not been abolished, it was reduced. Sub-national actors were accepting the fact that scattering funds for small-scale works was not conducive to effective regional development.

EU structural funds were expected to reduce the practice of clientelism after stress was placed on studies and long-term development. However, the deeper question was how this would affect the finer functioning of clientelism, and addressing it was quite challenging. Indeed, in many aspects this form of clientelism is nebulous. Considering the long history of clientelism in Greek politics, it was not expected that it would disappear completely as a method of interaction. It was still there, and it may always be there. However, it has changed and will continue to evolve. The changed structure and changed *politica* alter clientelism, but it remains as a method of interaction between actors of policy communities. This is where the concept of Mediterranean regime becomes useful. The assumptions are that there is a culture with distinctive characteristics that can be labelled Mediterranean; in the context of politics, this involves personalistic, informal, ad hoc methods of cooperation; and this interaction resembles a regime in that actors come together to secure collectively what they could not individually.

Players involved in EU structural policymaking were considered, as was their method of interaction and what they aimed to achieve. The expectation was that with decentralization there is an empowerment of peripheral actors, their conversion into partners, and the emergence of new forms of elite cooperation that resemble this Mediterranean regime. Although more research is needed, there is evidence of this type of relationship. More specifically, it was present in the regional committees and regional monitoring committees. The rationale indicates an understanding that to secure development in the region they must cooperate. Consequently, the division of responsibility was often blurred, and power was of less concern than in the past. The understanding of central actors was that sub-national partners were needed to secure comprehensive policy. The understanding of sub-national actors was that they must cooperate among themselves to secure their input in regional development.

Future: Towards What End?

On the basis of what senior officials in Athens stated during the period of this study, emphasis appeared to be shifting away from the prefectures. The central state accepted the need for decentralization, but future plans were somewhat ambiguous. Officials noted that they 'knew from where they came, but they did not know where they were headed.' The entire reform process was also very cautious. Officials in the Ministry of the Interior expected that a three-tiered system of sub-national government would be off the agenda. While the first tier was needed, the need for two additional levels of government was unclear. Further, if the third tier did become elected, the central administration would exist alongside it. The centre would not remain in its ministries, but it would be represented and would execute administrative responsibilities. Such a scenario, however, was not expected in the short term; rather, they were looking at a span of ten years (senior civil servants within the Ministry of the Interior). The reasoning was threefold: time was needed for the public to become accustomed to the idea of the *perifereia*; the centre wanted to test how administrative decentralization would function; and prefectoral actors were quite mobilized, so it would be difficult for the centre to abolish the prefectoral tier. This last aspect was particularly stressed. Indeed, prefects noted that second-level powers should be secured before reforms moved to the third tier. They argued that the respect for the principle of subsidiarity would give powers to the prefectures first and to the *perifereies* second. At the time, however, there were few demands stemming from regional secretaries. However, the focus of the central administration on the *perifereia* is not surprising. One could argue that this level corresponds to the geographic breakdown for the structural funds and hence there is logic in directing reforms to this level. But this does not explain why the prefecture was initially the focus of PASOK's reforms yet slowly receded to the background of its agenda. A more plausible explanation is that the central government was trying to diffuse the threat of the elected prefectoral councils by filling regional posts with a viable administration capable of implementing EU policy while under the 'control' of the centre. One can even argue that PASOK had a long-term interest in establishing a proper regional government at the *perifereia* and wanted to ensure that powers would not be usurped by the prefectures in the transition.

More than one decade lapsed since the last real set of reforms were implemented, and there were no significant changes in the regional structure. This cannot be explained solely by the change in governing party from PASOK to Nea Democratia in 2004, because there is still a gap with little change. It may well be that this was as far the Greek administration needed to go. That is, the 'fit' was better, hence the pressure to change subsided. This also supports the EU connection to the reforms. Following the widening of the EU to the east, there is also the question of the future of regional policy in Greece. The Commission is stepping back and is becoming less involved, ensuring the framework, and letting member states and their regions take over (interview with Commission officials). So sub-national actors may be losing their EU partner. If we consider Europeanization along a spectrum, there is the question of how far along the spectrum one must travel without fear of regression. Although it is still too early for a definitive verdict, the reforms are significant. The overall conclusion here is that there is evidence of strong Europeanization. There is an explicit Europeanization as is outlined in the legislation and is voiced by Greek actors themselves. There is also a covert Europeanization that is manifested in a learning that has created networks of cooperation that exhibit some elements of a Mediterranean regime. Finding an interaction with the characteristics of a Mediterranean regime in a country with such a long history of centralization is noteworthy.

Postscript

As this book is being prepared for publication, we are witnessing the turbulent turn of events in Greece and wider Europe. Measures addressing the fiscal crisis in Greece attempt to correct the problems long plaguing the Greek state.[1] This is Europeanization resulting from the pressures and demands of Euro-zone membership. Indeed, Greece is experiencing a new, aggressive form of Europeanization. It will be interesting to see how all this will be played out; we have the promise of unprecedented research.

Notes

Chapter 1

1 Most noteworthy are the contributions made by Andrikopoulou and
   Kafkalas (2004); Dimitrakopoulos and Passas (2004); Featherstone (2003,
   2005); Featherstone and Kazamias (2001); Getimis and Demetropoulou
   (2004); Ioakimidis (1993, 1994, 1996a, 1996b, 2001); Kazakos (1991, 1994);
   Papageorgiou and Verney (1992); and Plaskovitis (1994).
2 Börzel and Risse (2003); Cowles, Caporaso, and Risse (2001); Featherstone
   (2005); Featherstone and Radaelli (2003); Méndez, Wishlade, and Yuill
   (2007); Schmidt and Radaelli (2004).
3 The preamble to the Treaty of Rome (1957) stated that member states are
   'anxious to strengthen the unity of their economies and to ensure their
   harmonious development by reducing the differences existing between
   various regions and the backwardness of less favoured regions.' However,
   in the 1950s, the Community made only modest attempts to correct the
   regional economic disparities of its member states. It was expected that
   the market would undertake to balance the distribution of market factors,
   thereby gradually eliminating differences between geographically developed and underdeveloped areas. In 1975, the European Regional
   Development Fund was established. Small amounts of money were
   distributed to member states on the basis of a quota determined by the
   Council of Ministers. Although this indicated an increased concern about
   intra-Community disparities (Tsoukalis 1993), regional policy was still only
   a marginal policy and had limited impact on administrations and centre–
   periphery relations. There was a minimalism in that the European Commission wrote a cheque, and national executives used the funds for nationally
   determined projects (Hooghe 1996a, 1996c). Structural programs attempted

to shield the local level and bypassed the local tier. Indeed, implementation was left with member states, and no role was foreseen for either regional actors or for the Commission (Nanetti 1996).

4 The more comprehensive approach to development was first tested with the introduction of the Integrated Mediterranean Programs (IMPs). Shortly after Greece's accession into the European Community, Prime Minister Papandreou sought special treatment, claiming that Greece had 'economic peculiarities.' The IMPs were a response to these claims. They were intended for all of Greece and for the Mediterranean regions of France and Italy. Resources came from three structural funds: the European Social Fund (ESF), the European Regional Development Fund (ERDF), and the EAGG-F; and from the European Investment Bank (EIB). They were drafted in a small unit of the EU Commission (DGX VI) and were approved in 1985. The IMPs marked a new approach to regional policy (Hooghe 1996a, 1996c) because they stipulated that the programs be formulated and implemented 'at the relevant geographical levels' (Council Regulation EEC 2088/5). Further, they introduced the principles of subsidiarity and of partnership between Community, national, and regional authorities. Finally, they adopted a new approach based on medium-term development programs rather than on individual project submissions and a close coordination of different EC instruments and local involvement.

5 Loughlin (1997) identifies five types of regions: (1) economic regions, defined according to their economic activities (such as agriculture, industry); (2) historical/ethnic regions, with populations having a distinct historical, linguistic, or religious characteristics (Basques, Catalans, Scots); (3) administrative/planning regions – defined for purposes of administration, economic planning, or the gathering of statistics – which do not possess a democratically elected assembly to which the regional executive is accountable (Greek *perifereia*, in this study); (4) political regions, having regional governments accountable to directly elected regional assemblies (Spanish Autonomous Communities, Italian Regions); and finally (5) the Nomenclature of Territorial Units for Statistics (NUTS), by which the European Commission defines regions, which are simply the regional units of the member states and used for statistical purposes as well as for structural funds.

6 All translations are by the author, unless indicated otherwise.

7 The principle has its roots in the seventeenth-century writings of Johannes Althusius, whose work *Politica methodice digesta* focuses on multiple consociations where power is allocated to the lowest possible level or consociation. It is not, however, a means to delineate competencies

indefinitely; rather, the division of authority is a continuous political interaction where the allocation of competencies is continuously in question (Schaefer 1991). Subsidiarity is a principle that assumes a cooperative style of policymaking, one that favours the lowest level.

8 It was customary for central political elites at the time of modern European states to try to impose a unified order on territories regulated by varieties of local tradition and to try to create a homogenous entity. Modernizing elites believed that such practices as clientelism were an impediment to modernization and had to be abolished; its persistence indicated a dysfunctional political system, one that was not fully modern. An ideal type of integration involved penetration through the development of a loyal corps of civil servants who, through routine administration, would erode the power of independent communes and lords); standardization; and the institutional incorporation of the periphery (Tarrow 1977).

9 After independence from Ottoman rule, Greece followed an irredentist foreign policy. The *Megali Idea* was part of this plan to unify lost Greek territory. Indeed, in 1884, only 35 per cent of the present Greek state was part of Greece.

10 From as far back as ancient Greece, Cleisthenes created the *demos* or municipality in ancient Athens, which operated as a system of local government.

11 During the following year, 457 municipalities were created (three levels of city populations: over ten thousand, over two thousand, and under two thousand). Municipal councillors were directly elected, and mayors were elected by the council. Each council selected three candidates, of whom one was appointed mayor by the king or prefect, depending on the type of municipality.

12 This presents the question of how societies change – a topic addressed in later chapters, when the learning process that Greek political elites and civil servants are experiencing is examined.

13 They had exclusive taxing rights: slaughterhouses, pasture lands, drinking water, public weights and measures, cemetery privileges, parking facilities, oil lees, unbuilt real estate, beer, advertisements, building licences, lodgers and hotel guests, benefit from work carried out, town extension, changes in the town plan, lighting, pavements, squares, water supplies and irrigation, use of land and services, and waste disposal.

14 The work of Grémion (1976), Thoening (1973), and Worms (1966) on the political-administrative system showed that control of the central state was in fact a myth; there was a complexity in the French system, and Paris was mediated by local notables (*notables*).

15 The word is derived from the Greek *mesolavo*, which means 'I intervene.'
16 The study of patron–client relationships has increased remarkably since the 1960s (Eisenstadt and Roniger 1981). The explanation found even in economically developed (industrialized) societies led some academics to conclude that a modern bureaucratic state could be considered compatible with patronage (Lemarchand 1981; Mouzelis 1978; Piattoni 1997; Waterbury 1977). Piattoni (1997) identifies four types.of clientelism: virtuous, ineffective, vicious, and challenged. Virtuous clientelism results when cohesive patrons encounter strong opposition – this produces collective goods, growing legitimacy, and economic development. When patrons are divided and opposition is weak, the result is ineffective clientelism, which produces a distribution of individual goods, fading legitimacy, and economic stagnation. If we have cohesive patrons and a weak opposition, then we have vicious clientelism, with no output, no legitimacy, and no economic development. Finally, the combination of divided patrons and strong opposition produces challenged clientelism – symbolic output, eroded legitimacy, and economic involution.
17 List of interviews
   • Regional secretary of West Greece
   • Prefect of Achaia
   • Prefect of Thessaloniki
   • Upper-level civil servants in the *Perifereia* of Central Macedonia (seven interviews)
   • Upper-level civil servants in the *Perifereia* of West Greece (six interviews)
   • Upper-level civil servants in the Prefecture of Thessaloniki (five interviews)
   • Upper-level civil servants in the Prefecture of Achaia (four interviews)
   • Upper-level civil servants in the Ministry of the National Economy (eight interviews)
   • Upper-level civil servants in the Ministry of the Interior (twenty interviews)
   • Officials in the Regional Policy Directorate of the EU Commission responsible for the Greek Regional Programs, and other individuals in this directorate (twenty interviews)
   The regional secretary of Central Macedonia (1999) declined an interview, without explanation.
18 Their capitals, Thessaloniki and Patra, are respectively the second- and third-largest cities in population. The 2001 Census found the populations of Metropolitan Thessaloniki and Patra to be 1,057,825 and 210,494

respectively. The total population of C. Macedonia is 1,782,420 and that of West Greece is 741,282. Central Macedonia is in a key geographical position for the externalization of the Greek economy and the general geopolitical role of the country. The region comprises seven prefectures: Thessaloniki, Imathia, Serres, Chalkidiki, Kilkis, Pella, and Pieria. Thessaloniki is the capital city of Northern Greece and is referred to as the co-capital. It is one of the oldest cities in Europe, situated at the junction of national and international north-south and east-west transport routes. Its port, with its special Free Zone, provides facilities to other Balkan countries, has an important industrial complex, and is one of the most important centres for trade and communication in the Mediterranean. Patra also has a geographic advantage its harbour links the country with Italy (EU) and the Peloponnese with the Ionian Islands. Indeed, the port of Patra has a considerable cargo trade and is the largest port in Greece with respect to passenger movement. It comprises only three prefectures: Achaia, Ilia, and Aetolia-Acarnania. The *periferea* does not constitute a natural geographical or historical entity. Two of three prefectures – Achaia and Ilia – form a natural part of the region of Peloponnese and are identified historically, geographically, and culturally with this region. The Prefecture of Achaia is linked with Aetolia-Acarnania by bridge or ferry between Rio and Antirio. Achaia, however, has a long history and has played a dynamic role since 280 BCE, when the Achaian confederacy was created.

Chapter 2

1 In 1983, a constitutional amendment reduced the powers of the president (elected by the legislature) – powers that were transferred to the prime minister. This established a modified parliamentary system where the prime minister is vested with independent executive power.
2 Membership was also supported by the small centrist groups and the Communist Party of the Interior, which had Eurocommunist inclinations (Ioakimidis 1993). Those opposed to accession were the Panhellenic Socialist Party (PASOK) and the Communist Party of Greece (KKE). PASOK advocated direct democracy, self-management, regional autonomy, and popular mobilization, but these were not connected to Europe. PASOK did not want to compromise its socialist values by becoming part of Europe, for socialist parties of Europe were seen as too willing to accept capitalist ideology. Not surprisingly, Nea Democratia was behind the slogan 'We belong to the West,' while PASOK stressed that 'Greece belongs to the Greeks.'

3   Again, as noted earlier, this is not to argue that there was a one-way control in which the prefect controlled both the first tier and the prefectoral council meetings. This will be re-examined later in the book.
4   A top-down analysis reveals that there is a change in the relationship between national and sub-national authorities, which can be attributed to the challenges facing industrialized countries in general, and EU member states in particular (Bullmann 1997; Loughlin 1997). Indeed, in the 1980s, the region was rediscovered by political economists, political scientists, and sociologists (Storper 1997). Decentralization has taken place across much of Europe; reforming the structures of sub-national government can be seen as another attempt to modernize political systems and is a means of managing the overloaded administrative framework of the modern state (Bullmann). It can be argued that there is a trend towards regionalization and decentralization.
5   This involved cooperation between PASOK, the Nea Democratia, and Synaspismos.
6   Once again, the argument made here is that there is no connection between the elections of the prefectoral tier and the EU programs.
7   The Perifereiko Tameio was operational in 1998 at the same that all works were decentralized to the *perifereies*.
8   In 1994, there was a supplementary Law 2240 that provided for the Office of the Regional Administration. This office was headed by the regional director, who had responsibility at the prefectoral level – responsibility that had not been transferred to the prefectures (those not listed in Article 3/2218). The regional director also supervises the first-tier local government, similar to the way in which regional secretaries monitor the acts of the second-tier local governments. In 1997 the regional secretary assumed both tasks.
9   Direct elections of the prefects and prefectoral councillors took place for the first time in October 1994.

Chapter 3

1   Operational programs comprise specific development projects. CSFs, OPs, and SPDs are all forms of intervention (European Commission 1999a). They provide an analysis of the economic and social situation and the results of the preceding program period, a description of the strategy used, and financial tables summarizing the financial resources pledged. The 1988 reforms merged the European Regional Development Fund (ERDF), the European Social Fund (ESF), and the Guidance section of the European

Agricultural Guidance and Guarantee Fund (EAGG-F) under the label of 'Cohesion Policy.' For the 1989–93 programming period, funding came from these three funds. For the 1994–9 programming period (1993–9), a fourth fund, the Financial Instrument for Fisheries Guidance (FIFG), and a separate fifth fund, the Cohesion Fund, were added.

The ERDF is concerned with productive investment to permit the creation or maintenance of permanent jobs, investment in infrastructure, and endogenous development. The ESF is concerned with such matters as occupational integration of unemployed persons exposed to long-term employment, occupational integration of young people in search of employment, promotion of equal opportunities on the labour market, and strengthening education and training systems. The EAGG-F section deals with two types of measures. The first is linked to agricultural structures and seeks to support the start-up for young farmers, to improve the structural efficiency of holdings, to encourage the establishment of produc-ers' associations, and to improve the quality of agricultural products. The second group is concerned with measures that encourage rural diversifica-tion, which include the development of rural infrastructure, encouraging investment in tourism, and the protection of the environment and the countryside. The FIFG is not a Structural Fund as such, but it finances structural actions in the fisheries sector within the framework of Structural Fund programs. Finally, Cohesion Funding operates outside the Structural Funds, supporting environmental and transport projects for member states having a per capita GDP less than 90 per cent of the EU average. Recipient EU member states were Greece, Spain, Portugal, and Ireland.

2 The Ministry of Foreign Affairs and the Ministry of the National Economy play the most important roles in European matters; the Foreign Ministry has jurisdiction over external matters, while the MNE is responsible for internal coordination such as domestic issues and inter-ministerial coordination.

3 Once the thirteen *perifereies* were established, all the IMPs – with the exception of Crete – fell under the responsibility of more than one regional secretary.

4 The concept of planning was a 'novel notion for the Greek civil service,' a 'plunge into dark waters' (Papageorgiou and Verney 1992, 144; interview with a senior official in MNE on the IMPs and the pilot program of the IMPs for Crete). Planning relies on perceptions and practices that go beyond institutions (Spanou 1998). Greek sub-national administrations had no planning experience. Centralization and party politicization of decision-making, coupled with clientelist practices, did not provide sub-national

administrations the opportunity to develop a management capacity, expertise, or the necessary decision-making capabilities (Spanou). Central economic planning was introduced in 1964 in Greece, at the same time that the National Centre for Planning and Economic Research (KEPE) was established. It operated according to five-year plans, serving the needs of the ministries involved in economic development, particularly the Ministry of Coordination (later renamed MNE), which was responsible for drawing up the National Investment Program. These plans have been criticized for being over-centralized, providing mostly symbolic participation. Part of the problem was that KEPE was unable to get information from central and regional governmental departments and the fact that ministries were often reluctant to make medium-term planning and policy commitments.

5 The IMPs ended in 1992.

6 For the 1989–3 programming period, five objectives were assigned to the Structural Funds.

Objective 1 regions have a GDP per capita less than 75 per cent of the EC average, usually with a high percentage of the labour force in agriculture. This objective promotes development and structural adjustment of regions whose development is lagging. It encompasses four funds: the ERDF, ESF, EAGG-F, and FIFG. These regions include all of Greece, Ireland, Northern Ireland, Portugal, most of Spain, the Mezzogiorno, the overseas *départements* of France and Corsica, and in the post-1993 period, the new East German *länder*.

Objective 2 programs convert regions seriously affected by industrial decline. Eligibility is linked to an unemployment rate above the Community average, a percentage share of industrial employment exceeding the Community average, and a decline in this employment category. This objective draws from both the ERDF and the ESF.

Objective 3 combats long-term unemployment and facilitates integration into the working life of young people and of those excluded from the labour market. It is financed by the ESF.

Objective 4 facilitates the adaptation of workers to industrial changes and changes in production systems. It also draws from the ESF.

Finally, Objective 5 is subdivided into two areas. Objective 5a is geared to regions that need adjustment of their agricultural structures in the framework of the Common Agricultural Policy and facilitates the structural adjustment of the fisheries sector in the framework of the reform of the Common Fisheries Policy. It is funded by the EAGG-F and the FIFG. Objective 5b is aimed at the development and structural adjustment of rural areas. Eligible regions have poor socio-economic development (assessed on the basis of GDP per capita), and meet two of three additional criteria: a high level of agricultural employment; a low level of agricultural incomes; and a low population density and/or significant migration trends. It draws on the ERDF, the ESF, and the EAGG-F.

From the above, Objectives 1, 2, and 5b address regional development as such.

For the 1994–9 programming period, there was a sixth objective added to the five, which promotes the development of regions with an extremely low population. It was introduced to address the needs of Austria, Sweden, and Finland, following their accession in 1995. Funding for this objective comes from the ERDF, ESF, EAGG-F, and the FIFG.

7 This was the situation for other member state CSFs, which operated primarily in the framework of national strategies where the structure and definition of priorities was dominated either by sectoral considerations (Ireland and Portugal) or by regional planning considerations, as with the CSFs for Spain, Greece, Italy (the Spanish CSF concentrated on major basic infrastructure to improve internal networks and provide a link to Europe). The Greek CSF followed a diffuse strategy: it was highly integrated and there was synergy between measures, and it concentrated on medium and small infrastructure projects to reduce internal disparities and to improve living conditions in the regions.

8 The system of administration of the programs was outlined within the CSF. The MNE established the Epitropi Parakolouthisis (Monitoring Committee). There is a distinction between the Regional Council and the Monitoring Committee. The Regional Council comprises the regional secretary, prefects of all prefectures of the region, mayors of the largest city of each prefecture, interest group representatives, and the director general of the region, who is a non-voting member. Actors of the Monitoring Committee are the regional secretary as chair; prefects of all prefectures of the region; representatives of Local Union of Cities and Communities (TEDK); representatives of technical, commerce, unions (social partners); MNE, which acts as secretary of the Monitoring Committee; other Central Ministry officials; and representatives of EU DG XVI, V, VI.

9 The Commission, however, has promoted methods and tools through the Méthodes d'Evaluation des Actions de Nature Structurelle program. MEANS attempts to improve the methodological tools available for assessing structural actions. Member states are given eight criteria to use when assessing and producing the evaluation reports:

1. Meeting needs: Does the evaluation adequately address the information needs of the Monitoring Committee and fit the Terms of Reference?

2. Relevant scope: Are the program's rationale, outputs, and impacts fully covered, including unexpected outcomes?
3. Defensible design: Does the evaluation design answer the questions asked?
4. Data: Are the data that are used/collected appropriate and are their reliability duly taken account of?
5. Sound analysis: Is the information available subjected to appropriated analysis?
6. Credible findings: Do the findings follow logically from – and are they justified by – the analysis?
7. Impartial conclusions: Are conclusions fair, unbiased by stakeholder views, and operational?
8. Clarity: Is the report written in a way that is easy to understand? (European Commission 1999a)

Further, the guidance document, 'Common Guide on Monitoring and Interim Evaluations' (1996), published by the Commission, outlined that mid term evaluations should involve:

a critical analysis of all the data collected; some measurement of the extent to which objectives were being achieved; an explanation of any discrepancies between the actual and expected results of the intervention; and an assessment of the rationale for the intervention and the continued relevance of objectives.

10 The other explanation is that, in 1991, a special budget for public expenditure linked to Community funds was adopted. This ensured part financing of Community measures, thus eliminating one of the main reasons for unsatisfactory utilization of Community appropriations. Budgetary restrictions apply to other types of expenditures (European Commission, *Third Annual Report* 1991).
11 EAPTA is concerned with local self-government, involving works such as water supply, culture, tourism, competitiveness.
12 The regional secretary noted that the overall road of the program in 1995, compared to 1994, was very positive (Ministry of the National Economy 1998). Overall, during the two-year period 1994–5 the absorption rate of the programs was 52 per cent of the budget of public expenses, which was considered satisfactory, even though the program had a late start (approval from Commission 29 July 1994) (ibid.).

13 For example, problems in Subprogram 5 (Improving Human Capital), Measure 3, can be attributed to delays from the Ministry of Labour. Further, Subprogram 6, Support of Infrastructure of Local Self-Administration (EAPTA), Measure 2, displayed significant problems in completing works, because of delays in informing the Secretariat of PEP specifically on the progress of the economic and physical objectives of the works.

Chapter 4

1 In the case of regional policy, the Euro-sceptic stance is evident in the Greek government's obtaining exemption from European rules by including Attica as a region eligible for ERDF funding and later the memorandum that led to the IMPs (Andrikopoulou and Kafkalas 2004, 45).

2 Examples include Maria Damanaki, T. Bellos, B. Papageorgopoulos, I. Floros, I. Paraskeuas, P. Giannopoulos, Stamoulis, and further back Milt. Evert.

3 It is interesting to note that during the course of one interview, when an individual requested an application form, he was asked if he held a university degree. When he replied that he did not, he was told that there was no point in applying.

4 Smaller first-tier administrations have faced problems because they lack university experts and scientists. The public servants are not as well trained. Competent individuals have arrived and left.

5 The Ministry of Macedonia and Thrace (Northern Greece), established after the Second World War to show that the Centre cares about the periphery, is situated in the city. Papageorgiou and Verney (1992) had similar findings in the late 1980s and early 1990s with the IMPs.

6 In 1992, half the members were university graduates between the ages of thirty and forty-five.

7 Although this study did not include first-tier sub-national actors, evidence suggests that between 1994 and 1998, communities still needed prefects. What had happened in the past between the first and second tier now occurs between the first and third tiers. After 1998, the mayor's relationship with the prefect shifted to one with the regional secretary. The regional secretary has good relations with the mayors because the secretary needs the mayors to implement policies and the mayors need the *perifereia* for funding. After implementation of Law 2218, which merged local tiers and the strong municipalities, for local actors the *perifereia* has now become 'the state.' Not surprisingly, there are times when the prefect is either pressured or by-passed altogether (interview with Central officials and Commission officials).

Chapter 5

1 There is of course the possibility that administrative reform in regional
policy will eventually spill over into other areas of the administration.

Postscript

1 At the risk of over-generalization, we are looking at slashed pensions,
salary freezes, extraordinary levies, and steep increases in sales tax.

References

Andrikopoulou, Eleni, and Grigoris Kafkalas. 2004. Greek regional policy and the process of Europeanization, 1961–2000. In Dimitrakopoulos and Passas 2004, 35–47.

Armstrong, H., and J. Taylor. 1993. *Regional economics and policy*. London: Harvester.

Armstrong, Harvey. 1995. The role and evolution of European Community regional policy. In Jones and Keating 1995, 23–62.

Aucoin, Peter. 1996. *The new public management in Canada*. Montreal: Institute for Research Policy.

Auer, Astrid, Christopher Denmke, and Robert Polet. 1996. *Civil services in the Europe of Fifteen*. Maastricht: European Institute of Public Administration.

Averyt, William. 1975. Eurogroups, clientela, and the European Community. *World Politics and International Economies* 29 (1): 949–72.

Balme, Richard. 1995. French regionalization and European integration: Territorial adaptation and change in a unitary state. In Jones and Keating 1995, 167–88.

– 1997. Regional policy and European governance. In Keating and Loughlin 1997b, 63–76.

Balme, Richard, and Bernard Jouve. 1996. Building the regional state: Europe and territorial organization in France. In *Cohesion policy and European integration*, ed. Liesbet Hooghe, 219–55. Oxford: Clarendon.

Bateson, Gergory. 1973. *Steps to an ecology mind*. St Albans: Paladin.

Beetham, David. 1985. *Max Weber and the theory of modern politics*. 2nd ed. Cambridge: Polity.

Bellouber-Frier, Nicole. 1995. The case of France. In *National administrative procedures for the preparation and implementation of community decisions*, ed. S. Pappas, 227–300. Maastricht: European Institute of Public Administration.

Benz, Arthur. 1989. Intergovernmental relations in the 1980s. *Publius: The Journal of Federalism* 19:203–20.

Bollen, Frank. 1999. The reform of the EU structural funds: 10 questions on the magnitude and direction of reforms. *Eipascope* 1:2–10.

Börzel, Tanja A., and Thomas Risse. 2003. Conceptualizing the domestic impact of Europe. In Featherstone and Radaelli 2003, 57–80.

Boston, Jonathan, John Martin, June Pallot, and Pat Walsh. 1996. *Public management: The New Zealand model.* Oxford: Oxford University Press.

Bullmann, Udo. 1997. The politics of the third level. In Jeffery 1997b, 3–19.

Carney, Frederick. 1965. *The politics of Johannes Althusius.* London: Eyre and Spottiswood.

Christiansen, Thomas. 1995. Second thoughts: The Committee of the Regions after its first year. In Dehousse and Christian 1995, 34–64.

Christofilopoulou, Paraskevy. 1987. Decentralization policy in post-dictatorial Greece. *Local Government Studies* 13 (6): 6–15.

– 1996. Prefectural administration and self-government in the Greek political system. *Hellenic Review of Political Science* 7:124–53.

Cohen, Jean, and Andrew Arato. 1992. *Civil society and political theory.* Cambridge, MA: MIT Press.

Commission of the European Communities. 1991. *Third annual report of the implementation of the reform of the structural funds 1991.* Brussels: Commission of the European Communities.

– 1993. *Portrait of the regions: Portugal, Spain, Italy, Greece.* Vol. 3. Luxembourg: Office for Official Publications of the European Communities.

– 1997. *Annual report on the cohesion fund: 1996.* Brussels: Commission of the European Communities.

Constas, D., and T. Stavrou, eds. 1995. *Greece prepares for the twenty-first century.* Baltimore: Johns Hopkins University Press.

Cowles, Maria Green, James Caporaso, and Thomas Risse, eds. 2001. *Transforming Europe: Europeanization and domestic change.* Ithaca, NY: Cornell University Press.

Curtis, G.E., ed. 1995. *Greece: A country study.* Washington, DC: Library of Congress, Federal Research Division.

Daadler, Hans. 1966. Parties, elites, and political development. In *Political parties and political development,* ed. J. La Palombara, 43–77. Princeton: Princeton University Press.

Daoutopoulos, George. 1987. Community development in Greece. *Review of Social Research* 66:106–20.

– 1991. Community development in Greece. *Community Development Journal* 26 (2): 131–8.

– 1996. Prospects for community development in Greece. *Annals of Public and Cooperative Economics* 67 (2): 281–90.

Dehousse, Renaud, and Thomas Christian, eds. 1995. *What model for the Committee of the Regions? Past experiences and future perspectives.* Florence: European University Institute.

Dimitrakopoulos, Dionysis, and Argyris Passas. 2004a. Conclusion: Europeanization and the Greek policy style: National or sectoral? In Dimitrakopoulos and Passas 2004c, 139–47.

– 2004b. Greece: An introduction to patterns of EU membership. In Dimitrakopoulos and Passas 2004c, 3–15.

– eds. 2004c. *Greece in the European Union.* New York: Routledge.

Economic and Social Committee of European Communities. 1995. *Opinion on local development initiatives and regional policy.* Brussels: Economic and Social Committee of European Communities, 24–5 October 1995.

Eisenstadt, S.N., and René Lemarchand. 1981. *Political clientelism, patronage, and development.* London: Sage.

Eisenstadt, S.N., and Luis Roniger. 1981. The study of patron–client relations and recent developments in sociological theory. In Eisenstadt and Lemarchand 1981, 271–95.

European Commission. 1990. *Second Annual Report of the Implementation of the Reform of the Structural Funds 1990.*

– 1991. *Third Annual Report of the Implementation of the Reform of the Structural Funds 1991.*

– 1992a. *Fourth Annual Report of the Implementation of the Reform of the Structural Funds 1992.*

– 1992b. *An outline of community structural fund assistance in Greece.* Brussels: 11 March 1992. Memo 22/92.

– 1993. *Fifth Annual Report of the Implementation of the Reform of the Structural Funds 1993.*

– 1994. *The Structural Funds in 1994.* Sixth annual report.

1995. *The Structural Funds in 1995.* Seventh annual report

– 1996. *The Structural Funds in 1996.* Eighth annual report.

– 1997a. *Annual report on the Cohesion Fund: 1996.*

– 1997b. *The Structural Funds in 1997.* Ninth annual report.

– 1998a. *EU Structural Funds for Greece: Making good progress.*

– 1998b. *The Structural Funds in 1994.* Tenth annual report.

– 1999a. *Eleventh annual report on the Structural Funds in 1999.*

– 1999b. *Extracts from Objective 1 Community Support Framework 2 (SCF2) 1994–1999.*

– 1999c. *Mid-term review of the Structural Funds.*

– 2000. *Twelfth annual report on the Structural Funds in 2000.*

Economic and Social Committee of the European Communities. 1995. *Opinion on local development initiatives and regional policy.* Brussels.

Fatouros, Arghyrios. 1993. Political and institutional facets of Greece's integration in the European Community. In Psomiades and Thomadikis 1993, 23–42.

Featherstone, Kevin. 2003. Introduction: In the name of 'Europe.' In Featherstone and Radaelli 2003, 3–26.

– 2005. Introduction: 'Modernization' and the structural constraints of Greek politics. *West European Politics* 28 (2): 223–41.

Featherstone, Kevin, and George Kazamias, eds. 2001a. *Europeanization and the southern periphery.* London: Frank Cass.

– 2001b. Introduction: Southern Europe and the process of 'Europeanization.' In Featherstone and Kazamias, 1–22.

Featherstone, Kevin, and Claudio M. Radaelli, eds. 2003. *The politics of Europeanization.* Oxford: Oxford University Press.

Featherstone, Kevin, and George Yannopoulos. 1995. The European Community and Greece: Integration and the challenge to centralism. In Jones and Keating 1995, 249–67.

Flynn, Padraig. 1996. Adaptation of workers to industrial change: A new objective for the Structural Funds. Speech, Toulouse, 22 January 1996, EUROPA.

Gellner, Ernest. 1977. Patrons and clients. In Gellner and Waterbury 1977, 1–6.

Gellner, Ernest, and John Waterbury, eds. 1977. *Patrons and clients in Mediterranean societies.* London: Gerald Duckworth.

Georgiou, G.A. 1994. The responsiveness of the Greek administration system to European prospects. *International Review of Administrative Sciences* 60:131–44.

Getimis, Panayiotis, and Leeda Demetropoulou. 2004. Towards new forms of regional governance in Greece: The southern Aegean Islands. *Regional and Federal Studies* 14 (3): 355–78.

Gilsenan, Michael. 1977. Against patron–client relations. In Gellner and Waterbury 1977, 167–83.

Grémion, Jean-Pierre. 1976. *Le pouvoir Périphérique.* Paris: Le Seuil.

Hall, P.A. 1986. *Governing the economy: The politics of state intervention in Britain and France.* New York: Oxford University Press.

Héritier, Adrienne. 2001. Differential Europe: The European impact on national policy-making. In *Differential Europe: European Union impact on national policy-making,* ed. Adrienne Héritier, Dieter Kerwer, Christoph Knill,

Dirk Lehmkuhl, Michael Teutsch, and Anne-Cecile Douillet, 1–22. Boulder, CO: Rowman and Littlefield.

Hooghe, Liesbet. 1994. Building a Europe with the regions. Discussion paper no. 31. Oxford: Nuffield College.

- 1995. Subnational mobilization in the European Union. EUI working papers. Florence: European University Institute.

- 1996a. Building a Europe with the regions: The changing role of the European Commission. In Hooghe 1996b, 89–126.

- ed. 1996b. Cohesion policy and European integration. Oxford: Oxford University Press.

- 1996c. Introduction. In Hooghe 1996b, 1–24.

Hooghe, Liesbet, and Gary Marks. 1995. Channels of subnational representation in the European Union. In Dehousse and Christian 1995, 6–33.

Ioakimidis, P.C. 1993. Greece in the EC: Policies, experiences, and prospects. In Psomiades and Thomadakis 1993a, 405–20.

- 1994. The EC and the Greek political system: An overview. In Kazakos and Ioakimidis 1994, 139–53.

- 1996a. Contradictions between policy and performance. In Greece in a changing Europe: Between European integration and Balkan disintegration, ed. Kevin Featherstone and K. Ifantis, 33–52. Manchester: Manchester University Press.

- 1996b. EU cohesion policy in Greece: The tension between bureaucratic centralism and regionalism. In Hooghe 1996b, 342–63.

- 2001. The Europeanization of Greece: An overall assessment. In Featherstone and Kazamias 2001a, 73–94.

Jeffery, Charlie. 1997a. Conclusions: Sub-National authorities and 'European domestic policy.' In Jeffery 1997b, 204–19.

- ed. 1997b. The regional dimension of the European Union. London: Frank Cass.

Jones, Barry, and Michael Keating, eds. 1995. The European Union and the regions. Oxford: Clarendon.

Jouve, Bernard. 1997. France: From the regionalized state to the emergence of regional governance? In Keating and Loughlin 1997b, 347–69.

Kazakos, Panos. 1991. Hellada Anamesa Prosargmogi kai Perithoriopoiise: Dokimia Europaikis kai Ikonomikis Politicis. Athens: Diatton.

- 1994. Greece and the EC: Historical review. In Panos Ioakimidis 1994, 1–9.

Kazakos, Panos, and P.C. Ioakimidis, eds. 1994. Greece and EC membership evaluated. London: Pinter Publishers.

Keating, Michael. 1983. Decentralization in Mitterrand's France. Public Administration 61 (Autumn): 237–51.

- 1995. Europeanism and regionalism. In Jones and Keating 1995, 1–22.

– 1997. The political economy of regionalism. In Keating and Loughlin 1997b, 17–40.

Keating, Michael, and Liesbet Hooghe. 1996. By-passing the nation state? Regions and the EU policy process. In *Policy making in the European Union*, ed. J.J. Richardson, 216–29. London: Routledge.

Keating, Michael, and James Hughes, eds. 2003. *The regional challenge in Central and Eastern Europe: Territorial restructuring and European integration.* Brussels: Peter Lang.

Keating, Michael, and John Loughlin. 1997a. Introduction. In Keating and Loughlin 1997b, 1–13.

– 1997b. *The political economy of regionalism.* London: Frank Cass.

Keene, John. 1988. *Democracy and civil society.* New York: Verso.

Kernaghan, Kenneth. 1995. Keeping the new public management pot boiling. *Canadian Public Administration* 38 (3): 481–5.

Komninos, Nicos. 1998. *The innovative region: The regional technology plan of C. Macedonia.* Athens: Gutenberg.

Kristinsson, Gunnar Helgi. 1996. Parties, states and patronage. *West European Politics* 19 (3): 433–57.

La Palombara, Joseph. 1964. *Interest groups in Italian politics.* Princeton: Princeton University Press.

Ladi, Stella. 2005. The role of experts in the reform process in Greece. *West European Politics* 28 (2): 279–96.

Ladrech, Robert. 1994. Europeanization of domestic politics and institutions: The case of France. *Journal of Common Market Studies* 32 (1): 69–88.

Laird, Frank R. 1999. Rethinking learning. *Policy Currents* 9 (3–4): 3–7.

Lavdas, Kostas A. 1997. *The Europeanization of Greece.* Basingstoke: Macmillan.

– 2005. Interest groups in disjointed corporatism: Social dialogue in Greece and European 'competitive corporatism.' *West European Politics* 28 (2): 297–316.

Legg, Keith R. 1969. *Politics in modern Greece.* Stanford: Stanford University Press.

Leitner, Christine. 2000. Walking the tightrope: Cultural diversity in the context of European integration. *Eipascope*, 2000–1:20–4.

Lemarchand, René. 1981. Comparative political clientelism: Structure, process and optic. In Eisenstadt and Lemarchand 1981, 7–32.

Lemarchand, René, and Keith Legg. 1972. Political clientelism and development. *Comparative Politics* 4:149–78.

Loughlin, John. 1997. Representing regions in Europe: The Committee of Regions. In Jeffery 1997b, 147–65.

Loughlin, John, Eliseo Aja, Udo Bullmann, Frank Hendriks, Anders Lidström, and Daniel Seiler. 1999. *Regional and local democracy in the European Union*. COR studies. Brussels: European Communities.

Loughlin, John, and B. Guy Peters. 1997. State traditions, administrative reform and regionalization. In Keating and Loughlin 1997b, 41–62.

Lyrintzis, Christos. 1984. Political parties in post-junta Greece: A case of bureaucratic clientelism? *West European Politics* 7 (2): 99–118.

– 2005. The changing party system: Stable democracy, contested 'modernisation.' *West European Politics* 28 (2): 242–59.

Machin, Howard. 1977. *The prefect in French public administration*. New York: St Martin's.

Makridimitris, Ant. Perifereiakos Diefthindis. *Ta Nea*, 17 April 1996.

March, James G., and Johan P. Olsen. 1989. *Rediscovering institutions*. New York: Free Press.

– 1998. The institutional dynamics of international political orders. *International Organization* 52 (4): 943–69.

Marks, Gary. 1993. Structural policy and multilevel governance. In *The state of the European Community*, ed. Alan W. Cafruny and Glenda G. Rosenthal, vol. 2, 391–410. London: Longman Group UK.

– 1996. Exploring and explaining variation in EU cohesion policy. In Hooghe 1996b, 388–422.

– 1997. An actor-centered approach to multi-level governance. In Jeffrey 1997b, 20–38.

Médard, Jean-Françoise. 1981. Political clientelism in France: The centre–periphery nexus re-examined. In Eisenstadt and Lemarchand 1981, 124–71.

Méndez, Carlos, Fiona Wishlade, and Douglas Yuill. 2007. Made to measure? Europeanization, 'goodness of fit' and adaptation pressures in EU competition policy and regional aid. August 2007 European Policy Research Paper number 61, University of Strathclyde.

Metcalfe, Les. 1981. Designing precarious partnerships. In *Handbook of organizational design*, ed. P.C. Nystrom and W.H. Starbuck, vol. 1, 503–30. Oxford: Oxford University Press.

– 2001. The Maastricht Masters in European public affairs. *Eipascope*, 2000–1: 32.

Ministry of the Interior, Local Governance, and Decentralization. 1997. *To Kratos ton Politon*. Athens: Ministry of the Interior.

– 1998. *Sygrotisi tis Protovathmias Topikis Audodioikisis: Tomos A'*. Athens. Typographio.

– 1999. *Memo 4 February 1999*.

Ministry of the National Economy. 1990. *PEP: West Greece.* 1989–93.
– 1994a. *PEP: Central Macedonia.* 1994–9.
– 1994b. *PEP: West Greece.* 1994–9.
– 1996. *PEP: Central Macedonia: Report of the Monitoring Committee Teliki Ekthesi.*
– 1997. *PEP: West Greece, Report of the Monitoring Committee 4th Sinedriasi January.*
– 1998. *PEP: West Greece, Report of the Monitoring Committee Triti Ekthesi Axiologisi.*
– 1999. *PEP: Central Macedonia, Report of the Monitoring Committee, 6th Sinedriasi 1999.*
– 2000. *PEP: West Greece, Report of the Monitoring Committee Ekthesi Diachirisis.*
Mintzberg, Henry. 1996. Managing government, governing management. *Harvard Business Review* (May–June): 75–83.
Mitchell, James. 1996. Conservatives and the changing meaning of union. *Regional and Federal Studies* 6 (1): 30–44.
Moschonas, Gerassimos. 2001. The path of modernization: PASOK and European integration. *Journal of Southern Europe and the Balkans* 3 (1): 11–24.
Mouzelis, Nicos. 1978. Class and clientelistic politics: The case of Greece. *Sociological Review* 26 (3): 471–97.
– 1990. H Hellada sto Perithorio: Poios Ftaie? *To Byma*, 30 December 1990.
Nanetti, Raffaella. 1996. EU cohesion and territorial restructuring in the member states. In Hooghe 1996b, 59–88.
Olsen, J.P. 1996. Europeanization and nation-state dynamics. In *The future of the nation state*, ed. S. Gustavsson and L. Lewin, 245–85. London: Routledge.
Osborne, David, and Ted Gaebler. 1993. *Reinventing government*. London: Penguin.
Page, E.C. 1985. *Political authority and bureaucratic power: A comparative analysis.* Brighton: Wheatsheaf Books.
–   1995. Administering Europe. In *Governing the New Europe*, ed. J. Hayward and E.C. Page, 257–85. Cambridge: Polity.
Page, E.C., and L. Wouters. 1995. The Europeanization of the national bureaucracies? In *Bureaucracy in the modern state*, ed. J. Pierre, 185–204. Aldershot: Edward Elgar.
Papadopoulos, Kostas. 1997. Prefectoral self-rule: The road and developmental prospects of the legislation within the structure of administrative reform. 2nd Convention of ENAE.
Papageorgiou, Fouli, and Susannah Verney. 1992. Regional planning and the integrated role of Mediterranean programs in Greece. *Regional Politics and Policy* 2 (1): 139–61.

Pappas, Spyros. 1995a. The European partnership through national administrative procedures. In Pappas, 3–55.

– ed. 1995b. *National administrative procedures for the preparation and implementation of community decisions.* Maastricht: European Institute of Public Administration.

Paraskevopoulos, Christos. 2001. Social capital, learning and EU regional policy networks: Evidence from Greece. *Government and Opposition* 36 (2): 253–77.

– 2005. Developing infrastructure as a learning process. In *West European Politics* 28 (2): 445–70.

Paraskevopoulos, Christos, and Robert Leonardi. 2004. Introduction: Adaptational pressures and social learning in European regional policy – Cohesion (Greece, Ireland, and Portugal) vs. CEE (Hungary, Poland) countries. *Regional and Federal Studies* 14 (3): 315–54.

Pepelasis, Adamantios. 1989. The trends and prospects of the Greek economy. *European Affairs* 3, no 1 (1989): 85–9.

– 1997. Local political classes and economic development. In Keating and Loughlin 1997b, 306–46.

Peters, Guy. 1998. *Comparative politics: Theory and methods.* London: Macmillan.

Piattoni, Simona. 1997. Local political classes and economic development. In Keating and Loughlin 1997b, 306–46.

Plaskovitis, Ilias. 1994. EC regional policy in Greece: Ten years of structural funds intervention. In Kazakos and Ioakimidis 1994, 116–27.

Pollis, A. 1992. Greek national identity: Religious minorities, rights, and European norms. *Journal of Modern Greek Studies* 10 (2): 171–97.

Psomiades, Harry, and Stavros Thomadikis. 1993. Introduction: Greece at the crossroads. In Psomiades and Thomakikis, eds., *Greece, the new Europe, and the changing international order*, 11–20. New York: Pella.

Putnam, Robert. 1993. *Making democracy work: Civic traditions in modern Italy.* Princeton: Princeton University Press.

Radaelli, Claudio M. 2003. The Europeanization of public policy. In Featherstone and Radaelli 2003, 27–56.

– 2005. Europeanization: 'Solution' or 'problem'? Paper for the APSA Annual Meeting, Washington, DC, September.

Rhodes, R.A.W. 1985. Power-dependence, policy communities and inter-governmental networks. *Public Administration* 49:4–31.

– 1986. *European policy-making, implementation and sub-central governments: A survey.* Maastricht: European Institute of Public Administration.

– 1990. Policy networks: A British perspective. *Journal of Theoretical Politics* 2:293–317.

Richardson, Jeremy, Gunnel Gustafsson, and Grant Jordan. 1982. The concept of policy style. In *Policy styles in Western Europe*, ed. Jeremy Richardson, 1–16. London: Allen and Unwin.

Risse, Thomas, Maria Green Cowles, and James Caporaso. 2001. Europeanization and domestic change: Introduction. In Cowles, Caporaso, and Risse 2001, 1–20.

Samoni-Rantou, Catherine, and M. Zorbala-Walldén. 1995. In Pappas 1995b, 161–86.

Saurugger, Sabine, and Claudio M. Radaelli. 2008. The Europeanization of public policies: Introduction. *Journal of Comparative Policy Analysis* 10 (3): 213–19.

Savoie, Donald J. 1995. What is wrong with the new public management. *Canadian Public Administration* 38 (1): 112–38.

Schaefer, Guenther. 1991. Institutional choices: The rise and fall of subsidiarity. *Futures* 23 (7): 681–94.

Schmidt, Vivien. 1991. *Democratizing France*. Cambridge: Cambridge University Press.

– 2000. Democracy and discourse in an integrative Europe and globalizing world. *European Law Journal* 6 (3): 277–300.

– 2002a. Europeanization and the mechanics of economic policy adjustment. *Journal of European Public Policy* 9 (6): 894–912.

– 2002b. *The future of European capitalism*. Oxford: Oxford University Press.

Schmidt, Vivien, and Claudio M. Radaelli. 2004. Policy change and discourse in Europe: Conceptual and methodological issues. *West European Studies* 27 (2): 183–210.

Scott, James. 1977a. Patronage or exploitation? In Gellner and Waterbury 1977, 21–39.

– 1997b. Patron–client politics and political change in South East Asia. In *Friends, Followers, and Factions*, ed. S. Schmidt, 123–46. Los Angeles: University of California Press.

Sharpe, L.J. 1993. *The rise of meso government in Europe*. London: Sage.

Silverman, Sydel. 1977. Patronage as myth. In Gellner and Waterbury 1977, 7–19.

Smith, Andy. 1997. The French case: The exception to the rule? In Jeffery 1997b, 117–30.

Sotiropoulos, Dimitri. 1993. A colossus with feet of clay: The state in post-authoritarian Greece. In Psomiades and Thomadikis 1993, 43–56.

– 2004. Southern European public bureaucracies in comparative perspective. *West European Politics* 27 (3): 405–22.

Spanou, Calliope. 1995. *Penelope's suitors: Administrative modernization and party competition in Greece.* Discussion Paper no. 38. Centre for European Studies, Nuffield College.

– 1998. European integration in administrative terms: A framework for analysis and the Greek case. *Journal of European Public Policy* 5 (3): 467–84.

Stoker, Gerry. 1988. *The politics of local government.* Basingstoke: Macmillan Education.

Stone, Clarence. 1988. Preemptive power: Floyd Hunter's community power structure reconsidered. *American Journal of Political Science* 32 (1): 82–104.

– 1989a. Paradigms, power, and urban leadership. In *Leadership and Politics,* ed. Bryan Jones, 135–59. Lawrence, KS: University Press of Kansas.

– 1989b. *Regime politics: Governing Atlanta, 1946–1988.* Lawrence, KS: University Press of Kansas.

– 1995. Political leadership in urban politics. In *Theories of urban politics,* ed. David Judge, Gerry Stoker, and Harold Wolman, 96–116. London: Sage.

Storper, Michael. 1997. *The regional world: Territorial development in a global economy.* New York: Guilford.

Tarrow, Sydney. 1977. *Between centre and periphery.* New Haven: Yale University Press.

Thoening, Jean-Claude. 1973. *L'Ère des technocrats.* Paris: Éditions d'Organisation.

Thomadakis, Stavros. 1993. European economic integration, the Greek state, and the challenges of the 1990s. In Psomiades and Thomadakis 1993, 351–75.

Tocqueville, de Alexis. 1969. *Democracy in America,* ed. Jacob P. Mayer. Garden City, NY: Doubleday.

Tsarouhas, Dimitris. 2008. Social partnership in Greece: Is there a Europeanization effect? *European Journal of Industrial Relations* 14 (3): 347–65.

Tsinisizelis, M., and D. Chryssochoou. 1996. Images of Greece and European integration: A case study of uneasy interdependence? *Synthesis: Review of Modern Greek Studies* 1 (2): 22–33.

Tsoukalas, Konstantinos. 1979. *Greece and the European Community.* London: Saxon House.

– 1987. *State, society and labour in post-dictatorship Greece.* Athens: Themelio.

– 1993a. Free-riders in wonderland. *Hellenic Political Science Review* 1:9–52.

– 1993b. *The new European economy: The politics and economics of integration.* Oxford: Oxford University Press.

Vamvakas, Nancy A. 2002. Greece, the EU structural funds, and the emergence of Mediterranean regimes. PhD diss., University of Western Ontario.

Verney, Susannah. 1994. Central state–local government relations. In Kazakos and Ioakimidis 1994, 166–79.

Verney, Susannah, and Fouli Papageorgiou. 1992. Prefecture councils in Greece: Decentralization in the European Community context. *Regional Politics and Policy* 2 (1 & 2): 109–38.

Wallace, H. 1990. *The dynamics of European integration.* London: Pinter.

Waterbury, John. 1977. An attempt to put patrons and clients in their place. In Gellner and Waterbury 1977, 329–42.

Weingrod, Alex. 1977. Patronage and power. In Gellner and Waterbury 1977, 41–51.

Wenturis, Nikolaus. 1994. Political culture. In Kazakos and Ioakimidis 1994, 225–37.

Wishlade, Fiona. 1996. EU cohesion policy: Facts, figures, and issues. In Hooghe 1996b, 27–58.

Worms, Pierre. 1966. Le Préfet et ses notables. *Sociologie du travail* 3:249–75.

Wright, Vincent. 1994. Reshaping the state: The implication for public administration. *West European Politics* 17 (3): 102–37.

Yannopoulos, G.N. 1986. Integration and convergence: Lessons from Greece's experience in the European Economy Community. In *Greece and the EEC,* ed. G.N. Yannopoulos, 166–73. New York: St Martin's.

Zuckerman, Alan. 1977. Patrons and clients in Mediterranean societies. In Gellner and Waterbury 1977, 63–79.

European Union Studies

Catherine Gegout, *European Foreign and Security Policy: States, Power, Institutions, and American Hegemony*

Frédéric Mérand, Martial Foucault, and Bastien Irondelle, eds., *European Security since the Fall of the Berlin Wall*

Trygve Ugland, *Jean Monnet and Canada: Early Travels and the Idea of European Unity*

Nancy A. Vamvakas, *Europeanizing Greece: The Effects of Ten Years of EU Structural Funds, 1989–1999*